TELL A FRIEND

WORD OF MOUTH MARKETING:
How Small Businesses Can Achieve Big Results

ARNON VERED

arnon.vered@gmail.com

Designed by Rebecca Baldwin

ISBN-13: 978-0-6151-4775-8

The Tell A Friend Concept:

- About half of all businesses rely only on one marketing method: Word of Mouth Marketing.

- Big corporations are already using Word of Mouth (WOM) marketing as part of their marketing mix.

- To survive and thrive, smaller businesses need to learn from corporate best practices.

- Armed with WOM know-how, small businesses are more likely to be successful in WOM marketing because of their natural advantage: **A closer relationship with their customers.**

HOW TO READ THIS BOOK?

QUICK SKIM ||||▶
- ➤ You have the time and energy for about 20-30 minutes of reading.
- ➤ You want to quickly get a few ideas that you can immediately implement.

  - ☐ Go over the list of Word of Mouth marketing tactics on page vii (right after the acknowledgements page).
  - ☐ From the list, find chapters that you feel are the most relevant to you.
  - ☐ Spend a few minutes with those chapters:
    - ▪ Each chapter starts with "The Big Idea" section and ends with a "Chapter Summary-What you need to know" and "Exercises".
    - ▪ These sections are usually about a page long.
  - ☐ Do the right thing and try to spend at least a few minutes in Chapter 5 (Word of Mouth Ethics).

GETTING TO AN ACTION PLAN ||||▶
- ➤ You skimmed the book.
- ➤ You are ready to get into the details.

  - ☐ Spend a few minutes with the first section of the book: "Major concepts explained." It details the framework for Word of Mouth marketing.
  - ☐ Start spending more time with the "How to make it happen" sections in each chapter you find relevant to you. These sections provide the nuts and bolts of getting results using various Word of Mouth marketing tactics.

THE EXPERT ||||▶
- ➤ You are a business owner and Word of Mouth marketing is extremely important to your business.
- ➤ You are a marketing professional within an organization and need to be able to talk intelligently about all aspects of Word of Mouth marketing.

  - ☐ Finish reading the first section of the book: "Major concepts explained". Review the "What big corporations do" section in each chapter.

TABLE OF CONTENTS

ACKNOWLEDGEMENTS

First, I want to thank my wife Allie and my kids Joel and Sharon for their support in this project. Allie is also the book's editor. My readers: Rich Lehman, Glen Kirkpatrick, Dan Weintraub, Mike (Moshe) Benjamin and Peter Fishman, had some excellent points and were very insightful on how to make the book more readable. To Rebecca Baldwin, the designer of the book; you are a true artist. To my colleagues at Bain & Company and Capital One, the knowledge I have gained from you is the foundation for writing this book. Finally, to the extended Vered family in Israel, the Irvine family in Canada and our great community and friends in Richmond Virginia, thank you for your continued encouragement.

Arnon Vered
arnon.vered@gmail.com

TABLE OF WORD OF MOUTH MARKETING TACTICS

SECTION I

**The 30-Minute Primer –
Major Concepts Explained**

1 INTRODUCTION

The Big Picture:

Word of Mouth (WOM) is the most important weapon in many businesses's marketing arsenal. A Gallup poll found that 45 percent of businesses in the United States rely *solely* on WOM marketing. Big corporations recognize the potential of WOM, and have at their disposal large marketing budgets used to create smart and sophisticated WOM campaigns. Even so, smaller businesses have the upper hand when it comes to WOM because they can get up close and personal with their customers and potential customers. The "local" nature of a small business creates WOM opportunities corporations only dream about. To turn opportunity into success, small businesses need to take a page from the corporate WOM best practices manual. More thought and more discipline around WOM can yield tremendous results.

Why businesses should read this book:

As a consultant at Bain and Company and later as an analyst and a manager in Capital One's Small Business department, I have seen WOM evolve from a collection of ideas into a more coherent discipline. Corporations are quickly adopting it, and almost every business owner I talk to wants to know about it. Quantitative studies show that WOM is extremely important to business growth; but if you ask owners or marketers about their WOM strategy, the usual answer is, "I hope it happens!" People are confused about how to "do" WOM marketing. While many small businesses pay attention to online marketing, they have questions like, "Do I need a Blog? What kind of online presence should I have?" They also know how important face-to-face conversations are in driving WOM, but admit that they don't have a clear strategy on how to translate those into WOM. Finally, many owners know that referrals are a big part of their business, but are not sure how they happen.

I have learned through years of marketing to businesses that each business has a unique story and structure. Yet, as a business practice, WOM is one of the few practices that apply to every enterprise. This book will address basic WOM concepts and offer a menu of tactics every business can apply for immediate results. Including:

- Take a behind-the-scenes look at what corporations are currently doing in various WOM campaigns.

- Teach you how to engage more people to talk more positively about your business *and* encourage them to reach out to more people.

- Show you how you can employ a variety of devices currently used in the industry, both on and offline, to develop WOM.

- Provide clear suggestions on how to get started on WOM, including more advanced methods as well.

Why is this book different than other WOM books?

Most WOM books currently on the market are directed at big corporations. Many focus on creating massive success through buzz and viral techniques. Others discuss who to target in these campaigns (e.g. Evangelists versus Influencers). Most of the cases and tactics used in these books are not very applicable to businesses that are not big corporations. Another major disadvantage of these books is that they are full of corporate jargon. That's okay for internal presentations to company VPs, but doesn't connect with those working outside the boardroom. Finally, there are some specific books about creating Blogs for buzz marketing. Considering that I recommend the creation of Blogs for some businesses (albeit a small number), but don't go very deeply into 'how-to', these books are a great complement to *Tell a Friend*. Big corporations continue to daydream about runaway WOM success stories (VW bug, iPod, the Blair Witch Project, to name a few). Small businesses, I believe, crave a guide that offers a holistic approach to WOM that is realistic about what can be achieved locally with little to no marketing resources.

(i) Keep this page handy, we will
refer to it throughout the book.

WORD OF MOUTH
MARKETING FRAMEWORK

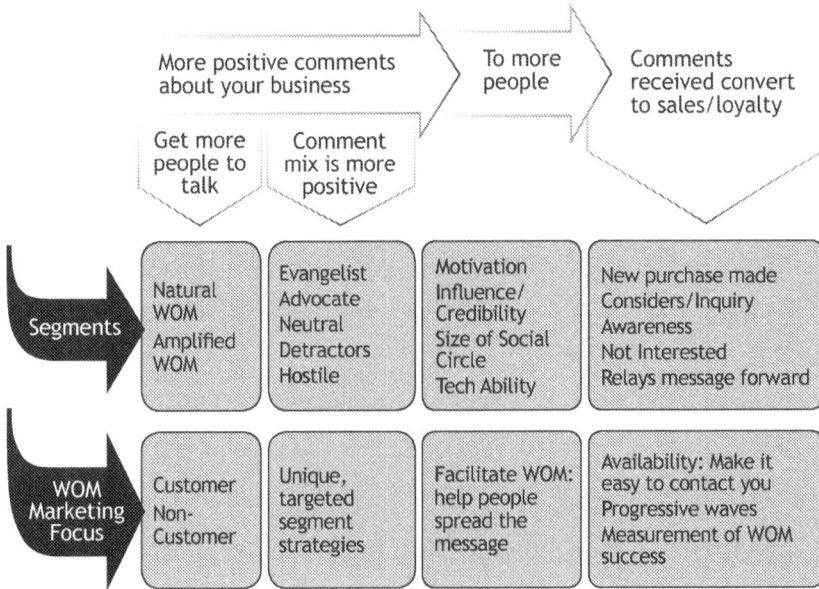

More positive comments about your business		To more people	Comments received convert to sales/loyalty
Get more people to talk	Comment mix is more positive		

Segments	Natural WOM Amplified WOM	Evangelist Advocate Neutral Detractors Hostile	Motivation Influence/ Credibility Size of Social Circle Tech Ability	New purchase made Considers/Inquiry Awareness Not Interested Relays message forward
WOM Marketing Focus	Customer Non-Customer	Unique, targeted segment strategies	Facilitate WOM: help people spread the message	Availability: Make it easy to contact you Progressive waves Measurement of WOM success

2 INTRODUCING WOM MARKETING

Why do people talk?

We talk because we are humans. We talk for an endless number of reasons: to impress, to inform, to seek advice, and to share. In this information era, people spend a significant amount of time talking about products and services.

Basic concept: **People talk about products and services.**

There are four business-related topics people talk about:

- Planning to make new/recurring purchases.
- Their shopping experience.
- Experience using a current product/service.
- Reaction to marketing and advertising.

Comments can have various attributes:

- Level of promotion:
  - ▶ From persuading someone to buy a product, all the way to discouraging them from trying it. Some comments are fairly promotion neutral (e.g. telling someone about a funny ad).
- Emotional investment:
  - ▶ Some people talk so passionately about a product they purchased that it sounds as if they were involved in making it.
- Importance of topic:
  - ▶ For a homeowner, choosing the right contractor for major home renovations is a far more important conversation than what is the best kind of grass seed.

- Fact versus opinion:
  - ▸ Many people share their strong opinions about the environmental effects or labor practices of various products and companies, but they often don't know all the facts (some of these topics are very complex). On the other hand, some products (e.g. financial services) elicit more fact-based conversation and may be relatively opinion free.
- How comments were received:
  - ▸ Was the message understood? Was the receiver of the message influenced? Did the message leave some lasting impression?

Amplified Versus Natural WOM

Amplified WOM

Basic concept: Encouraging people to talk about a product or service. Amplified WOM happens when a marketer tries to encourage more people to make more positive comments about a product or service. A marketer can launch a *WOM marketing campaign* or include a *WOM marketing component* for various other business activities. To use some simple examples: a business owner can start an email campaign and encourage people to forward it to their colleagues (*WOM campaign*). A business owner can launch a new product keeping in mind what could be 'conversation worthy' about it (the *WOM component*).

Natural WOM

Basic concept: Conversations are part of the normal course of business. Natural WOM is defined as conversations that are a result of the normal course of business that are not driven by a specific WOM campaign. Your business, your product and the way you interact with your customers are already a topic of conversation for some people.

There is no clear distinction between Natural and Amplified WOM. Almost every Natural WOM conversation is a result of some business decision. When referring to Amplified WOM, I usually talk about deliberate action businesses take to increase the volume, positive message and reach of WOM.

Many people ask, "Isn't Natural WOM enough?" It might be if your business is in the enviable position of not requiring growth or continued loyalty. However, if sustaining your business and growing it *is* on your mind, the thesis of this book is that you should invest some time amplifying WOM.

The Overall Goal of WOM Marketing

> *Definition:*
> Increase sales and loyalty by increasing the volume
> of positive comments about your business.
>
> - In WOM marketing, you aim to get more people to talk about your business more positively to as large a pool of people as possible.
> - Those positive comments, in turn, need to persuade the listeners to make new purchases, or to strengthen their ties to a product or service they already buy.

Customers and non-customers alike can be the targets of WOM marketing, but may require different strategies. Customers, and sometimes non customers, can be divided into categories ranging from "hostile" to "evangelist" in the Endorsement Spectrum. All together, they can be placed into five buckets: Evangelist, Promoter, Neutral, Detractor and Hostile. WOM begins with an understanding of who these consumers are and what their needs are.

When a person is ready to begin spreading the word about your business, their ability to do so is determined by four key factors: their motivation, their status as credible experts or influencers on the topic, the size of their social circle, and, finally, their technological abilities. A person who is an Evangelist for your product is extremely motivated to promote it. An Evangelist who has a large circle of friends who trust her, and who promotes your product to her email list and in her Blog, is the Holy Grail of WOM. More realistically, approaching Promoters (those who willingly say good things about a business) with a reasonable social circle and motivating them to pass information along is where most WOM marketers usually start.

To encourage people to talk to a larger number of people, WOM marketers try to help facilitate those conversations by providing samples of the product to people to give to their friends, sending emails that can be passed along, or simply giving people business cards/flyers they can distribute. Compensating people to encourage them to talk is one possible approach; but that kind of WOM marketing strategy requires much thought and research (tactics like this can backfire if people learn that WOM is being paid for).

For each segment or combination of segments on the Endorsement Spectrum, a unique set of strategies can be employed to help you begin achieving your WOM goals, including more conversations, more positive comments, broader reach and greater conversion.

Like every marketing effort, the Return On Investment (ROI) – an increase in sales/loyalty versus investment in time, technology, cost – needs to be comparable to or better than other marketing options. Prioritization is always a focus for time and cash-strapped business owners. For the 45 percent of businesses that rely exclusively on WOM marketing, the choice is between various WOM tactics.

Get more people talking about your business

The basic premise of WOM marketing is to get more people to talk about your product or service. Traditional advertising tries to maximize reach – counting the number of eyeballs reading a newspaper ad or the amount of direct-mail envelopes opened. Similarly, the first step in building WOM reach is to increase the number of 'human media outlets' for your business.

Ensure the mix of comments is more positive

Positive WOM: Building great products, providing superb service, and listening intently to customer concerns and delights form the basis of positive WOM. The idea behind WOM marketing is that while marketers try to influence people to talk more about their business, they also try to influence the message that will be repeated to the next person or group of people down the line. For example, while a contractor provides a good or service, he might also tell his customers about his commitment to working with Habitat for Humanity. He anticipates that his investment as a volunteer will be rewarded by current customers because they will relay this information about him to others, increasing the likelihood that he will be talked about in a positive way.

Neutral WOM: Not only positive comments count; neutral comments are important as well. Big corporations spend a significant amount of effort on 'brand building'. TV, magazines, and online ads are used to achieve this goal. In brand building, corporations are not trying to sell a product per se, but to 'soften' potential customers so that when they are ready to make a purchase, they will remember that specific brand. When a dentist opens a clinic in a new neighborhood and goes to talk to a local group about the latest in oral hygiene, she hopes to create some 'buzz' about the new doctor in town. People might talk about the quality of the presentation and their overall (non medical) impression; but since the clinic has just opened, they are unlikely to make positive or negative comments about the dental service itself. The bottom line is that if new appointments are made because people heard about the presentation (even neutral comments), the WOM marketing goal has been achieved.

Negative WOM: Negative comments may be the most important of all. If people have a complaint about your business or service, they are more likely to complain to others than to you. Your ability to identify what upsets people about your product or service will allow you diminish the domino effect of negative WOM. Positive WOM can gradually build a business; negative WOM can quickly sink it. Businesses cannot afford any negative WOM blind spots and need to devise strategies to "search and destroy" problems continuously.

More comments reach more people

Motivating others to pass information along is the most important method in spreading WOM. Once somebody is motivated to comment on your product or service to a larger group of people, the success of the campaign will depend on that person's credibility (on the topic) and status as Influencer, as well as the size of their social circle and their technological ability to spread the word.

Motivation: First, a person needs to feel motivated to say something positive about a product. This goes back to the question of why people talk. In this case, the level of motivation to deliver the message will not just affect whether a comment is made, but also how many comments will be made and to how many people. Motivation is not black and white. We all have things we want to tell the whole world about and other things that we very rarely mention.

Credibility/Influencer: We are all experts in something. People are likely to listen more to those they perceive as credible on certain topics. They also listen more attentively to people who are usually 'tuned in' and are considered Influencers. Influencers can range from prominent media personalities who can spark WOM campaigns with a single review, all the way to regular folks who are more persuasive and trustworthy than average on certain issues. The fact that we are all experts in something means that all of us can claim to have status as an Influencer in some area, or at least we have the potential to be one.

Social Circle: You are who you know. Clearly, you want the person saying good things about you to contact the largest number of people (warm leads, if possible). The fact that a person has a large social circle does not necessarily mean that he or she will tap into that pool of people on your behalf. What's important is that the *potential* is there. A business usually wants to invest more time in a person who has the potential to reach more people.

Technological Ability: The most important development in WOM marketing in the last decade has been technological advancement. Far beyond the old-school, over-the-fence conversations of yesteryear, today a bewildering array of methods exist to communicate opinions quickly to a large group of people. In the past, the water cooler was an important venue for those seeking advice about products, and a place for them to share their frustrations or excitement about their experiences as consumers. Back then, when people's thoughts were not widely distributed, corporate marketers had a lot of power. That power is rapidly diminishing.

The corporate stranglehold on messaging began to weaken with the advent of cell phones. Suddenly, shoppers could get recommendations on the run. Then email allowed people to share their views with a network of friends, and friends of friends. Personal websites and Blogs allowed consumers to publish their opinions for everybody in the world to read. Peer-to-peer communication, such as chat rooms and instant messaging (e.g. MSN Messenger), facilitate the dissemination of ideas even further. With all of these advancements, the concepts of Influencer and social circle changed radically.

Human "connectedness" is still increasing. Social computing is the latest phenomenon. People of all ages spend time daily making "friends" on websites like Myspace, bebo and Facebook. For professionals, it's Linkedin. All of these websites make it easy for people to network with people they already know, and to share information with people they don't know at all (but have something in common with). The bottom line: consumers and businesses are adopting these technologies at a very fast pace. What's even more important is that they expect to be able to share their thoughts with an even wider audience and are hungry for the opinion of others.

We are Getting More Connected

Technological Development in Communications Effect
Our Ability to Share Opinions

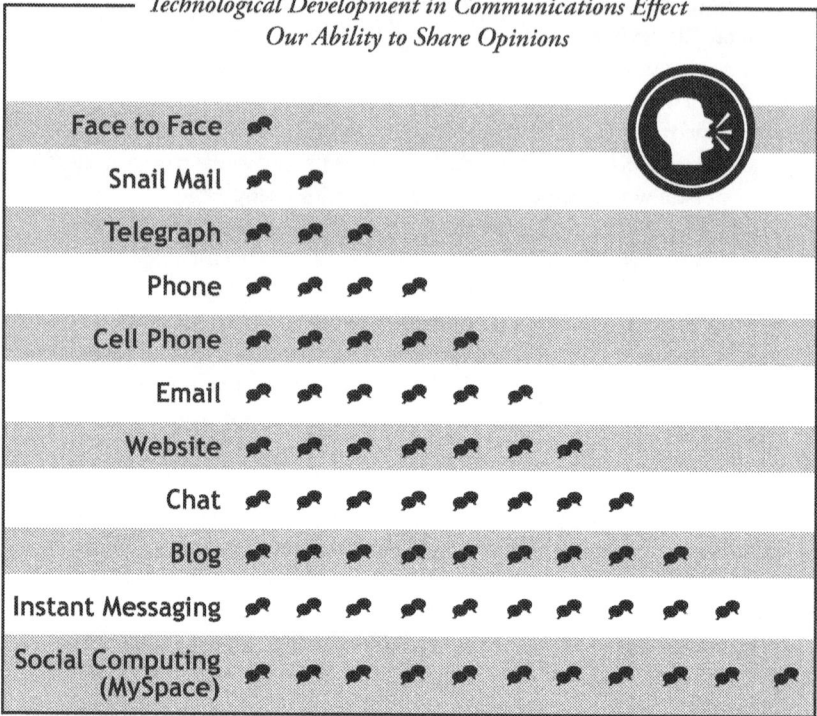

Face to Face	
Snail Mail	
Telegraph	
Phone	
Cell Phone	
Email	
Website	
Chat	
Blog	
Instant Messaging	
Social Computing (MySpace)	

3 WOM POPULATION SEGMENTS

Customer versus non customer

A successful WOM marketing campaign should target both customers and non customers. Indeed, customers may not always be your primary choice in WOM marketing. In fact, many start-up businesses have few or no customers, but still want to use WOM to break out. Furthermore, customers may not be the most influential or credible, or they may lack the social circle and technological abilities to effectively spread the word out about you. You definitely need to have *some* strategy involving customers, but cracking the code on WOM marketing for non customers may present a superior benefit/cost ratio.

When people decide to talk about you, they first ask themselves the question, "What's in it for me?" For customers, a sense of loyalty and satisfaction (or, alternatively, anger) about your product might drive at least some natural WOM. Loyal and satisfied customers are probably going to be more likely to follow up on your amplified positive WOM marketing campaigns. Non customers present a more complex situation. Without an actual experience with you, they need to be persuaded that passing information about you along to others makes sense. In Section II, we will dive into various ways to encourage non customers to talk positively about you.

The Endorsement Spectrum

| Evangelist | Promoter | Neutral | Detractor | Hostile |

- **Evangelist:**
  - ▸ First coined in this context by Ben McConnell and Jackie Huba in their book *creating customer evangelists.*
  - ▸ Definition: People who volunteer to be your constant sales force. Religious or cult-like following. Talk about your product often and try to convert people to it. In popular media, Evangelists are usually described in connection with new, cool, elusive or limited-access products. Think Tivo or Nascar.
  - ▸ Downside: How many products and services can you credibly evangelize? Evangelists can have significant impact, but the chances of finding clients who are sufficiently emotionally involved to promote your business this way might be limited.

- **Promoter:**
  - ▸ Promoter, Neutral and Detractor definitions became popular by Fred Reichheld, a partner at management consulting firm Bain & Company, in his book *The Ultimate Question.*
  - ▸ Definition (of Promoter): People who, in response to the question "would you recommend this product to a friend (on a scale of 1-10)?" answer nine or ten. They may not go out of their way to promote you, but given the opportunity, would probably do so. The key to turning customers into Promoters is providing them with great products and superior service. Reasonably speaking, this is the group you want to focus most of your effort on. Given the right treatment and solid "talking points," they will be energized to do WOM marketing on your behalf.

- **Neutral:**
  - ▸ Definition: Would give your business between a 3 to 8 on the "recommend to a friend" ratings scale. Not as involved as Promoters, but if some of their buttons are pushed the right way, might pick up a cause or two. Can they be turned around? Is there a chance they will still mention you positively in a conversation? They are certainly worth your effort. While there are many companies/services I am indifferent to, if the opportunity arose, I might still mention them positively at some point (e. g. recommend a local business I've had experience with over a national chain).
  - ▸ Non customers: It's likely that most of your non customers will fall into this group. It is very feasible that you will be able to convert some neutral non customers into Promoters, or even Evangelists through WOM marketing or other methods.

- **Detractors:**
  - ▸ Definition: If they are your customers, they answered one or two to the "recommend to a friend" question. If they are not your customers, they might have heard negative WOM about you. Even worse, when given a chance, they might try to persuade others not to try, or to stop using your products or services.
  - ▸ Strategy: Unless your Detractors are very vocal and are telling you or any

other touch points you have with them (e.g. customer service) about their concerns, you might be missing out on a key piece of business intelligence. Seek out Detractors and discover why they think you are not up to par (mild) or should be shunned (more extreme). One of the key concerns bigger companies have about opening a Blog or an online message board is that they provide an open forum to Detractors. However, companies that have dared to go through this exercise and even engaged their Detractors in a constructive conversation (e. g. Ford Motor Company) have discovered that their demons are actually fairly reasonable people who had solvable problems that the company was pleased to learn about and address.

- **Hostile**
  - ▸ Definition: Will try their best to take you down. Whether they are customers or not, this group is thinking vengeance and maximum damage. An example of Hostile WOM is environmentalists who focus on product boycotts because of the environmental harm companies cause or because of animal testing. Customer complaints about bad corporate citizens or poor service find their way to newspapers, Blogs and websites. Almost every corporation has a rogue anti-company site. To get a glimpse of this phenomenon, go to any search engine and type a name of a well-known company and the word suck; hit search and you'll be surprised with how much is out there.
  - ▸ Hostiles should be avoided at all cost, but unfortunately they are also a part of doing business. No matter how hard you try, you will not always get it right, and some people are always going to be offended by something.
  - ▸ Engaging them in a conversation that can diffuse their hostility might be possible, but requires careful message planning.

Putting it all together using the framework:
Unique, targeted segment strategies

The goal of WOM marketing is always the same: get people to talk about you in order to drive more business. In today's corporate WOM industry, there are a variety of niche companies that each champion a limited set of tactics. Some are very focused on Influencer programs. Others facilitate two-way conversions between businesses and consumers, while still others can tell you the number of comments made about you in Blogs and how positive were they. The list goes on. The point here is that all these tactics work for some businesses in some segments. The key challenge presented by WOM marketing is that, with each marketing/advertising/PR company pushing its brand of WOM as *the* WOM, the casual observer can easily get confused about what's relevant to each one of their business's segments (e.g. Customer vs. Non customers; Promoters vs. Neutrals).

Let's dive into an example to explain how you can use the segmented approach in a WOM marketing framework. Mrs. McGraw, a Real Estate agent, opened up shop about two years ago in a developing suburb of a mid-size city.

She has some clients, but is looking aggressively for more business. She will have to explore customer and non customer WOM marketing tactics. Because she is relatively new to the business, non customers probably don't have any opinion about her, unless they were already exposed to some natural WOM. Mrs. McGraw hopes that many customers *were* creating positive natural WOM and that this would result in more business. However, she knows that she needs to take some action to amplify and facilitate WOM in order to grow. Natural WOM will not be enough to achieve her goals.

Her customers can be clearly categorized using the Endorsement spectrum. She knows that at least in five deals her customers were very satisfied, so she might have some Promoters. She believes that her performance on other deals was just 'okay' and that the impression she left means that those clients can be categorized as Neutrals. Her relationship with her customers has given her some idea about which of them has a big social circle. She is aware that issues like credibility or tech know-how are not that relevant: Most people buying or selling a house serve as a credible source when it comes to talking about a Real Estate agent's performance. Nobody is going to create a website or Blog about her services. Her focus is local, and she expects most conversations about Real estate agents to be low tech (phone or email). She is also not giving up on her goal to encourage non-customers to begin conversations about her. To make that happen, she will have to try some 'out of the box' amplified WOM tactics.

Mrs. McGraw has mapped out her segments. She can now move on to evaluating the various tactics she can employ with each one of them. The key question on her mind is which segment will have the biggest impact on her business and how many tactics can she realistically execute on.

Facilitating WOM: Helping people spread the news

For every combination of Natural or amplified WOM tactics and segments, you will need to come up with an idea on how to help people transfer your message to others. In fact, the ability to facilitate the delivery of the message might be a key factor in your decision which tactic to employ. Stories about you are much more likely to be passed on if they are short and memorable. One example using technology might be to create some unique information on your website and send the link to customers who will, in turn, forward it to build an email chain. Many websites have a 'Refer a Friend' button. Others can even make it 'cool' to transfer information by creating funny videos. The reason online WOM is so hot is that messages and information can be shared quickly and efficiently to large groups of people.

For many Small Businesses, however, the online revolution (excluding email) still **means little** to their WOM marketing activities. I expect many people holding this book feel this way. The offline world (plus email) still holds many opportunities to facilitate WOM that businesses have not yet explored.

There are four aspects to facilitating WOM:
- *Physical aspect* is what you can give people to give to their friends: Business cards, coupons, pamphlets, videos, books, and so on.
- *Story aspect* is something unique and conversation-worthy about your business. It might be the way you promote your business or your unique personal story. It may be a 'wow' moment in your customer service, or anything that gives people a reason to make conversation.
- *Motivation aspect* is about what's in it for the person starting the

conversation. It goes back to the question of why people talk. They can talk because they are being supportive of you (your current relationship, something special you have done for them, or favors they plan to ask in the future). It could be that you have provided them with some unique or even personal information that makes them feel "in the know". They may be talking because sharing information about you makes them look smart or knowledgeable. If you want your message to spread like wildfire, you need a clear answer to the question why you believe people will be motivated to talk about you.

- *Viral aspect* is a function of how easy it is to move the message forward to many people. Email has a very strong viral aspect to it. A face-to-face conversation can also have high Viral potential if the person you talk to has a large social circle and is likely to repeat your message to many people.

It is important to re-iterate that Natural WOM is not generated by incentives like cash or trade. One should be very careful about designing an incentive-based WOM marketing scheme. You want incentives to be an addition to your WOM marketing efforts, rather than the main focus. The basic principle is this: People must be willing and motivated to talk, but a reward can potentially seal the deal. People should not have the opportunity to seriously 'game' the system. They should also not feel cheapened by a perceived effort to make them into sales vehicles. More details appear in the Refer-a-Friend (Chapter 14) and Your buzz team (Chapter 16) sections.

Facilitating WOM is segment sensitive. If there is a way to promote you, Evangelists will find it. How about Neutrals? You will probably have to do a lot more work on them before they will be willing to make the effort and talk about your business to others. Every WOM tactic chapter discusses specific ways to facilitate WOM.

Comments convert to sales/loyalty

The ultimate goal of WOM marketing is to achieve business results. Positive comments must lead to action. The reasons why some comments lead to action and others don't are the same reasons every marketing campaign can succeed or fail. The person making the reference has to be credible and persuasive. The message needs to connect with the receiver and be relevant to their circumstances.

Broadly speaking, the person that hears comments about your business has four options:

- To make a new purchase.
- To consider it, or ask for more information.
- To decline interest.
- To relay the message to others (creating more WOM).

To facilitate conversion, businesses must maintain a high level of

availability; they must be easy to find. In case receivers also want to continue sending the message to more people, business owners need to think about how to support and facilitate these **progressive waves of WOM**. Finally, regardless of tactics, business owners must **measure** success.

Availability: When someone hears that you do a great job, they will want to find you. Advanced planning ensures that the search is quick and easy. Make sure your name and number appears in the Yellow Pages or other multiple listings both offline and online. The growing trend is the local versions of Google and Yahoo (e.g. Yahoo local). There are many other sites to consider, depending on the industry (some of the bigger ones are craiglist and ebay). Businesses should also consider other forms of advertising that can keep them top of mind. Permanent signs that are visible from busy roads, strategically located posters, or even an ad in a book/guide people are likely to keep on hand make good investments. Other forms of advertising can function as reminders. To be sure, for many businesses, advertising supports their major marketing effort (WOM) and not the other way around. See the 'WOM in the marketing mix' (Chapter 20) for more on this.

The best strategy to enhance your "availability" is to incorporate your contact information into the WOM message. For example, if you give out samples for people to pass along, or you design an email that people can forward (WOM facilitation), be sure that your name, phone number or website are included. Do you really need your own website for this purpose? Not necessarily. While today websites are easy to create, even for non techies, you need to ask yourself (or better yet, survey a few customers or peers) if a website will make it easier for people to find you. For many businesses, being on some form of multiple listing (like Yellow Pages), or having people giving out their contact information as part of the WOM exchange is sufficient.

Progressive waves of WOM: It's easy to get swept away with the math. If I talk to ten people and each of them talks to ten people, by the ninth round we will have reached a billion people (ten to the power of nine). The world has seen examples of extraordinary WOM growth with products like iPods or Google; everybody was talking about them. This kind of 'Tipping Point' (Malcolm Gladwall's bestselling book) massive success is something most of us might read about, but never actually experience with our own businesses.

It is realistic to expect some progressive waves of WOM. You can anticipate them in Natural WOM, or even moderately successful amplified WOM campaigns. People who learned about you (not from you) can potentially continue to pass the information along to at least a few others.

Measurement – Evaluating WOM: "How did you hear about us?" If you can ask that question and keep track of the answers you receive, you are off to a great start. Before you begin planning a WOM campaign, it is important to understand your existing Natural WOM. Doing so might also offer some clue to the success of your WOM marketing efforts down the road. The basic element of WOM is that it's unpredictable and unregulated. WOM marketers have to accept that ambiguity. The bottom line is that asking people how they heard about your business and potentially *what* they heard about your business creates the ultimate feedback loop: If your campaign works, you will be able to discern if people heard about you because of some action you took.

SECTION II

Small Business WOM
Marketing Strategies

5 THE ETHICS OF WOM MARKETING

Achieving the goals of WOM marketing is hard work. It is not easy to control *how* people talk about you. Unfortunately, some businesses, big and small, deceive the public with inauthentic WOM campaigns. Not only is this tactic just plain wrong, it can backfire, placing the company's or individual's reputation in danger. I am sure you have been to websites where people can post comments about a product. Have you ever noticed that, on some sites, the comments champion a product in a way that looks suspicious? If you discovered that a company was asking employees to go online and pose as customers, your perception of the brand would plummet.

Surveys show that WOM is trusted more than any other form of advertising. I would hope so. If we can't trust the people around us more than the media, our society is in big trouble! Given that small businesses have an advantage when it comes to WOM marketing, it is in their best interests to keep it that way.

The Word of Mouth Marketing Association (WOMMA) has picked up this cause by continuously campaigning for ethical WOM. WOMMA has done an excellent job in defining the positive philosophy of WOM marketing, as well what can be considered deceiving or unethical actions. I used their WOM 101 (available online at *http://www.womma.org/wom101.htm*) as the basis for the below, with translations from corporate speak.

WOMMA insists that an ethical WOM campaign is an honest one:

① Honesty of relationship: Explain who you are speaking for.

② Honesty of opinion: Say what you believe.

③ Honesty of Identity: Never obscure your identity.

This, of course, refers both to you, your employees, and the people you are hoping will speak on your behalf.

Word of Mouth Marketing has positive goals:
- Creating a great reputation.
- Talking *and* listening to customers and non customers.
- Giving people something to talk about.
- Encouraging people to talk.

Word of Mouth Marketing **should not** be:
- Shilling: Paying people to talk about your business (offline and online) without disclosing that you hired them.
  Example: Businesses paying people (sometimes even actors) to 'talk up' their product in various places (standing in line at the bank or at student centers).
- Fake identities: Promoting your product in online forums, websites or Blog comments using a fake identity. Similarly, it is unethical to make negative comments about competitors in this fashion.
- Fake or misleading information: Communicating inaccurate or exaggerated information about your product, your company or yourself.
  Example: Posting comments on your own product in online communities (such as eopinions.com) that misrepresent its true value.
- Non-permission marketing: A receiver of information must either already have a relationship with the sender, or agree in advance to receive information.
  Example: It's okay for somebody to send an email to all their friends with a product recommendation. It's not acceptable to send an email to a distribution list without any knowledge about its members and whether the information would be relevant to them (otherwise known as spamming).
- Marketing to children: The self-enforced age limit in the WOM industry is 13. I strongly object to companies who try to market to kids hoping that they will, in turn, persuade their parents to buy big ticket items (like cars or TVs). I also oppose incentivizing kids to persuade their friends to buy kids-themed products. Children will continue to observe advertising that is or is not directed at them. I believe that there is a clear line separating ads that focus on brand building and campaigns that push kids to either talk to people outside of their age group or incentivize them to talk to their friends.

Simply put, the more Amplified WOM marketing campaigns resemble Natural WOM, the more ethical they are. The vehicles of ethical WOM marketing are customers and those who've had a chance to sample a product in some way (or, at minimum, have heard about it). WOM marketing channels people's motivation to spread positive comments about a product they like. It also encourages companies to be unique, to create great products, and to provide superb customer service. All these elements make a business "conversation worthy".

The principles above hit on what many smaller businesses consider their core values. Because of their size, many businesses can form one-on-one relationships with their customers, making them instantly aware of problems they face and, most importantly, help them to feel special. Smaller businesses can forge a "personal bond" with their customers, and that relationship *defines* the Small Business Advantage. Customers of smaller businesses are more likely to patronize them, to share their vision and to promote them to others. Keeping WOM ethical is essential to protecting this advantage.

Chapter Summary – *What you need to know*

- ☑ WOM marketing's positive focus is creating great reputations, listening and talking to customers, and giving them something to talk about.

- ☑ WOM marketing should not include: Using fake identities, using fake or misleading information, spamming or marketing to children.

- ☑ You, your employees, helpful friends and family should all follow these guidelines.

- ☑ WOM is the most trusted media. It is our responsibility to maintain that trust.

REPUTATION IS EVERYTHING

The Big Idea

Most business owners believe that their reputation is the main source of natural WOM. They are right. We all want businesses to deliver on their promises, and then some. Not even the most brilliant ad campaign can overcome lousy products or a bad customer experience. The beauty of the competitive market is that people have options. They can decide whether or not to patronize a company. They also have the power to tell others about their experiences. If you are committed to providing the best product or service available, you will get some natural WOM from your customers. Comments will become increasingly more positive as you gain more Promoters, and perhaps even Evangelists. People will be more motivated to support your cause and tell more people about it. You will also be able to start thinking about amplifying WOM. A great reputation can really get a WOM snowball rolling.

What Big Corporations Do

Big corporations and great reputation are words not usually found in the same sentence, especially when it comes to marketing practices. TV ads with impossibly fine print, disclosures ("customer agreements") that even lawyers can't understand, an endless stream of 'bait and switch' tactics: These are what we've come to expect. Products can also be disappointing. Companies cut corners on safety and durability, and promote "self help" (read: no help) customer service. Even Apple, whose reputation seems impeccable, has received severe public scrutiny for the short life of batteries in its flagship product, the iPod.

Companies start to notice the effect of these issues when they can connect them to their bottom line. And they do. For the last several years, companies have been focusing on the public aspects of a bad reputation. Various remedies can be found in the public domain as well: Public relations, press releases and new product or service promises. In the credit card world, Citibank heavily advertised a 'simplicity' card that promised an immediate, live customer service representative. Pharmaceutical and tire companies react quickly with recalls when a safety problem arises, before government can coerce them to act. Reputation management has long been front and center.

Companies also acknowledge the growing power of consumers' influence, or WOM. Before, companies had to worry about what the media reported. Now, it's all about consumer-generated media. Consumers are significantly more effective in sharing their views on a product via email, comments on various websites (Eopinion, Cnet, Myspace to name a few) or if they are die-hard techies, their own website. Companies want to react, but they can't directly influence or censure what people are saying (given that they accept ethical boundaries). If they want to effect the conversation, especially if it's negative, they have to join it. For example, GM's blog 'Fast lane' is written by one of its executives and tries to address common concerns and complaints about the Michigan behemoth. It gives a human face to the company and uses non-corporate language that fits this medium of conversation.

When it comes to WOM and reputation, companies are not just thinking defense, but also offense. When companies believe that their reputation is great, or at least better than their competition, they begin to think about the advantages they can gain from positive WOM. They don't want to stop with the natural WOM that might be generated either from customers or non customers. They want more people to talk more positively to even more people about their great products and services. This explains the growing interest in active WOM marketing.

Making It Happen

Customer Focus Versus 'Running the Business'

'Customer focus' sounds like the biggest buzz word in the biz. It is what every corporation professes, but few succeed in delivering. For smaller businesses, on the other hand, this illusive goal is actually achievable. They are often closer to their customers and understand them better. Corporations disperse knowledge of their customers between market research, brand, product information and a share of some senior manager's time, preventing any real understanding or "ownership" of their customers.

Businesses must have a razor-like focus on the quality of the product they deliver to the customer and the customer's experience. There are many distractions when running a business (e. g. cash flow, employees, suppliers), so balancing 'running the business' with keeping track of customer experience is a challenge. Even so, it is the key to building your reputation.

Set Expectations, Keep Your Promises

Setting clear expectations and delivering on your promises: These are the fundamental building blocks of a business's reputation. Some businesses over promise and under deliver. When customers are frustrated, they are less likely to advocate for you and negative WOM can result. It's clearly better to make reasonable promises and over deliver. This strategy is a surefire reputation builder. Doing things faster than expected or including more bells and whistles ensures a positive customer experience. At the same time, something as simple as an extra phone call inquiring about customer satisfaction or adding a personal touch to service can achieve tremendous results. For example, a business might promise to fix something in five days knowing that, on average, it takes them about three. Reputation-building is incorporated into the sales pitch. Over delivery is one of the best reputation builders out there. Search for ways to achieve this goal that are not difficult or expensive.

Listen to Customers and Re-evaluate Your Business Practices

Put on your listening ears and find out what customers think about you. 'Listening', more formally known as 'market research', can happen in many ways (see 'Two-way Conversation', 'Measurement' and 'Negative WOM' chapters for a more in-depth discussion). The principle remains the same: Understand people's concerns, frustrations, and delights when it comes to your business. People will have reactions to every aspect of your business -- from advertising to service calls. Make sure that when you ask for feedback, keep it broad or have a good idea of what are your key strengths and weaknesses are. Understanding what customers and potential customers are thinking about should lead to action. However, not every comment is worthy of action. Judgment and some cost/benefit analysis should always prevail. Acting to make things better is not just a way to build a great reputation (that by itself should lead to Natural WOM); it is also the basic research you need in order to build an effective Amplified WOM campaign.

Advertising

If you are actually doing advertising, don't do what some corporations do (over promise, remain vague about actual product features, include lots of fine print). Instead, be explicit and clear. Use straight-forward language that people generally use when they talk about your product. Those in the marketing profession know it's the trend, and it also makes sense. As a small business, you are more likely to understand the frustrations and delights of your customers and potential customers. Use that information to guide every communication.

Reputation with Partners

To build your business and get ahead, you rely on various partners. Banks, suppliers, accountants, lawyers, and employees are perhaps the most common examples. Building a great reputation with them is important by itself, but can also create unexpected synergies with your customer acquisition and retention efforts. Partners are a great source of first-wave natural or amplified WOM. These groups often have direct interaction with your customers and can help build and develop your positive image. You want them to be singing your praises at every opportunity.

Amplified WOM

One of the goals of Amplified WOM is reputation building. It is the business equivalent of corporate reputation management. Most businesses don't send out press releases or talking heads to TV interviews; but when they employ Amplified WOM tactics, they are shining a light on the best, most conversation-worthy areas of their business. Amplified WOM also addresses any shortcomings or concerns people might have about the business.

Small businesses can't afford reputation 'issues', especially when the enterprise consists of only one person (as is the case for more than a third of businesses in the United States). There may be some isolated negative events that need addressing (see discussion below), but as a whole, the goal of Amplified WOM is to build on a great reputation. With increasing consumer power (more competition, more ways for customers to share their views), progressive businesses are aware of the importance of their reputation and are willing to invest in making sure it is never in jeopardy.

Negative Event

When a negative customer experience occurs, you have to correct it quickly. The cliché 'the customer is always right' is more powerful today than ever before. In our Internet era, the adage reads more like: 'The customer is always right and if you do something wrong, they can tell the whole world.' Increased customer power presents a sort of carrot and stick conundrum. When in doubt about how to react to a nagging customer complaint, make sure to keep that in mind.

Chapter Summary – *What you need to know*

☑ A great reputation is the main source for natural WOM.

☑ To achieve a superb reputation that will lead to WOM, businesses need to:

- *Maintain a razor-like focus on what their customer's actually experience (product, service, etc) even when 'running the business' is time consuming and complex.*

- *Set expectations about what they will deliver and keep their promises.*

- *Continuously listen to customers and re-evaluate business practices, when appropriate.*

- *If using advertising, be explicit and clear.*

- *Build their reputation not only with customers, but also with suppliers, contractors, partners, and professional services.*

- *Make sure that if a customer has a negative experience, it is quickly addressed. The effects of negative WOM can be devastating.*

Exercises

- ☑ Try to map the common sequence of events your typical customers follow (initially call to find out more details, hold a first meeting, order, call for service, etc). You can do this by asking a customer or just as a thought experiment. Try to answer the following:
  - *Do you feel you actually understand what your customers go through in each step (is a certain step inherently confusing, stressful, quick, etc)?*
  - *For each step identified, think about what you can do to make their experience better. Conceive of several ideas, then prioritize and implement.*

- ☑ Write down three instances in which you know your customers have had a bad experience, and three instances where you have had a bad customer experience with some other company:
  - *What can you do to avoid these in your business?*
  - *What would make things better?*

7 YOUR STORY, YOUR FIRST STEP

The Big Idea

Companies exist because of what they make or what they do. Some company activities are conversation worthy, while others are not. What every business and business owner has, however, is a story. Maybe it's about how they started, their background, or about who uses their products. There are many things outside the realm of the actual product or service the company produces that serve as very important WOM generators. The advantage of developing and promoting your story is that it creates awareness of your business. It may cause people to notice you, to check you out, or maybe later consider becoming a customer. Depending on the story and how people empathize with it, you may also convert Neutrals into Promoters and create second-wave WOM. Story WOM is not necessarily tied to new sales, but can be a key element in creating the building blocks of sales: Awareness and consideration.

What Big Corporations Do

Corporations strenuously promote appealing and consistent stories about their history and what they stand for. It's called branding. To maintain their image, they also pepper the media with various narratives that support their brand or company story. That's called public relations. While many brands focus on product as their defining element, others focus on the more inspirational aspects of their history to attract attention and generate WOM.

A great story, for example, on how the company started, is not meant to just entertain the people who hear it; its goal is to be interesting enough to be repeated to others. Take Google. How many times have you heard that Brin and Page started the company in a garage when they were university students? A few years back, this provided great material for articles in every newspaper on Earth. The story captured people's imagination, and they happily consumed it and repeated it to others. Google had a great product to start with, which is the basis for any WOM campaign, but their story lent itself to WOM and catapulted their brand to new heights.

Big companies are often plagued with issues that one-person-companies rarely even think about. They are bureaucratic and are governed by policies that are hard to understand. Various groups handle a customer through the business relationship and there is no one person taking 'ownership' of a customer. If you ever have a conversation with somebody who works in marketing strategy in a corporation, ask them when was the last time they talked to a customer directly (outside of a focus group, other market research activity or a friend/family).

Zeroing in on a company's story creates the image that it stands for something greater than its unharmonious parts. Take State Farm, for example. Like most big insurers, they are sometimes criticized for their customer service, cumbersome claims process and prices. In response, State Farm TV ads focused on the personal stories of customers who enjoyed one-on-one service from their agents. One State Farm agent helped a customer who sunk his car in a lake. The agent also happened to be a diver, so he actually helped pull the car out of the water. Such a memorable story creates the image of a service provider as helpful neighbor, and achieves the company's goal of distancing itself from the mundane, sometimes frustrating details involved in dealing with a big insurer.

A Few Examples:

Example: Founder's Story	
Message	On September 7th, 1998 Google was commercially launched from a friend's garage.
Context	Launch of Google.
Between the lines	We may look like a big company, but we understand the little guy – we were there once too.
Reality Check	They already had $1 million in capital when the garage-based company started.

Example: Product Development	
Message	In 1971, Bill Bowerman stared into his breakfast waffles and saw a better way to make running shoes. As he poured rubber into his wife's waffle iron, he started a running revolution.
Context	Launch of Nike's massively successful product: The modern running shoe.
Between the lines	Our ideas don't start in laboratories. We get our hands dirty and keep it real.
Reality Check	Nike outsourcers the production of shoes. The company's main focus is design and promotion.

Example: Founders' Character	
Message	As long as you're thinking, think big.
Context	Donald Trump
Between the lines	Experience the legend when you buy a Trump property or gamble at a Trump casino.
Reality Check	While busy filming episodes of "The Apprentice", Trump's 'Trump Casino & Hotel Resorts Inc' restructured under bankruptcy protection.

Example: Failure/Success	
Message	Our favorite holding period is forever.
Context	Warren Buffet's famous long-term investment strategy.
Between the lines	Trust our decisions, invest in us.
Reality Check	He is for real. On the day this was written, Buffet announced a $30-billion gift to the Bill and Melinda Gates Foundation, the largest-ever charitable donation.

Smaller businesses have a tremendous advantage over big corporations when it comes to using their story to create and promote WOM.

The small business story advantage

- **One-on-one relationship built in.** In order to communicate their brand through a story, a large corporation must make a substantial investment in advertising or public relations. Headquarters struggle to control the story while communicating it on a mass scale. Smaller businesses, however, often communicate directly with their customer. A personal exchange lends your story credibility, and makes it meaningful and memorable. We watch many ads, but its not every day that somebody tells us about themselves. Big corporations understand that talking to clients individually is ideal. Their business-model economics and scale usually don't allow for that, giving smaller businesses a clear advantage.

- **Believability.** Hearing a story from the lips of a human being is always going to be more credible than a TV ad or a newspaper article based on a press release. There is widespread skepticism about corporations (nurtured by the likes of Enron and WorldCom, and too-good-to-be-true advertising). In the case of small businesses, a story does not have to mask corporate inadequacies. It is simply a way to connect to the listener and encourage his or her support.

- **WOM Marketing.** Corporations often try to push their stories through various media outlets. Their hope is that the narrative will be memorable enough to enhance their image. For the reasons mentioned above, I would argue that big businesses have a lower rate of success in encouraging people to tell these stories to others (WOM marketing) than small businesses. When a SB owner tells a customer their story, they make that person feel special. After all, the owner is taking the time to share something of themselves and make a personal connection. If positioned well, a story can make listeners feel like they have exclusive insight to a story not many people know. They will pass that story along for the same reasons that rumors and gossip are shared: Information is social currency.

Making It Happen

Find Your Story

What is your story? What is unique and conversion worthy about you or your business? To get people talking about you, you will need to develop a few "sound bytes" or anecdotes that are likely to be repeated and that put you in the best light. These stories need to somehow capture the imagination, and be unique, special or different. You can motivate people to talk about you because they empathize with you. Or maybe it's something special that you have done. There are many reasons people talk. Use your knowledge of your audience (who they are, what they care about, who they talk to) as a guide. In fact, it's always a good idea to have several stories that you can pull out of your hat, depending on the circumstances.

Here are a few guidelines to help you start crafting your story:

- **Personal:**
  - ▶ What did you do before you started the business? Is there something unique in your past?
  - ▶ How did you start the business? What inspired you? Why are you in business?

- ▸ What else do you do apart from the business (hobbies, passions, community involvement)?
- ▸ Causes that you support or "do-good" initiatives that you've been connected to.

- **Business:**
  - ▸ Past successes, failures or important turning points in your life and business.
  - ▸ Changes in your business model or offering.
  - ▸ Do you have any story-worthy customers or business partners?
  - ▸ Is there something unique about your business model? For example, the way you interact with customers?
  - ▸ Have you had unique or odd experiences while managing your business?
  - ▸ What have you learned from running the business?

- **Your business identity:**
  - ▸ Many businesses think long and hard about their vision, mission statement, and values. Done well, they operate like a strategic compass and explain to customers (and employees) why the company is exceptional. It is easy to fall prey to well meaning but generic descriptions. If you are one of those lucky companies that have nailed down a captivating business identity, use it to your advantage. Research and common sense lead me to believe that people will patronize and promote a company that offers good value, and knows where it's heading and why.

Talk to the people who are closest to you to generate ideas. They can help guide your thinking while identifying your story highlights. You can also tap into your extended network and customer base. Ask them what stories they have told friends or family about you (over and above your actual product or service).

Whatever story or stories you decide on, make sure that they can be told in a *short* period of time. If the story requires significant background and detail, it won't get passed around. Think about how much airtime you give yourself when you tell a story about a fellow business person. Politicians are trained to make their point in a TV-ready 30 seconds or less. That's probably good advice for business stories as well. The goal of the story is to be memorable and show you in a positive light. Short stories can definitely achieve this goal.

Push Your Stories

To make your story work as a WOM igniter, you have to tell it. Sounds simple? Not at all. With a zillion things on your plate, trying to create the right moment to share your story with anybody is not easy. Partial solution: Try to make it *part of your routine*. Where does story telling fit in your regular course of business? Do you have ample airtime to make your initial sales pitch? Or, at the other end of the spectrum, do you have time to converse in your post-sale discussion (e.g. a contractor that has finished doing some home renovation). Redirecting the conversation to talk about yourself may prove awkward.

Think about it this way: When people work with a small business, they expect results. They also expect a personal touch and a camaraderie that is far from the assembly line approach of big business. When you tell your story, you are fulfilling customer expectations of a small business.

Don't be shy about telling your story and make sure others aren't either. You, your employees, and those you talk to need to feel a sense of urgency about passing it on. You need to make repeating it a habit, and motivate your employees to follow suit. I can't emphasize this enough! Be as proactive about WOM as you would any other business practice. You will soon see dividends.

A personal, one-on-one relationship with whoever listens to your story will have several implications. First, when people get to know you better, they are more likely to become your customers and continue to be loyal afterwards. There is a difference between a business transaction and a relationship. Buying bread from a supermarket versus a local one-person bakery shop is not the same experience. Your loyalty to the latter (given that the quality/price combination is reasonable) will be higher. Second, a relationship usually entails a higher likelihood of promotion by your listener. In other words, the chances of positive WOM (specifically, your story) spreading, is higher.

If you have a well-defined and meaningful business identity (vision, values, mission statement, logo, and so on) that is truly unique, you need to make sure it consistently appears in all your communications. First, you and your employees should strive to embody that identity. It should also form the basis for your strategy and action plans. Second, think about how you address the outside world, whether its people inquiring about your company, current customers, partners or suppliers. Your message about what your company stands for and how you are planning to carry out that mission must be crystal clear, consistent and mentioned often. Thirdly, all other forms of communications should have some representation of your business identity. Think about how you present your story as part of brochures, letters and emails. Also think about scripted phone conversations, like when a prospective customer calls for more info or a customer service call.

Know Your Segments

As a small business owner, you will need to develop a story that will work with each segment. Customers might be better targets for more personal stories and will be more comfortable hearing and passing those stories along. Non-customers are more likely to be interested in material regarding your professional life or business. Try to get a sense of where people fall on the Endorsement Spectrum. If they are Neutrals, what will entice them to start talking about you? If you feel that your audience is Promoters or Evangelists, try a story that is more (unabashedly) self promoting.

For each group, but especially Promoters and Evangelists, you will need to evaluate their motivation to talk to more people and their credibility, size of social circle and technical ability. Clearly, those who are more motivated or who have a better ability to spread the word around should get more attention and focus. What this means is that you will need to make a special effort to create the right circumstances for your sharing. In other words, think about the return on the time you've invested and try to maximize it.

Facilitating 'Story WOM'

Facilitating 'Story WOM' is all about encouraging people to talk about you. You need to decide how to actually communicate the story (Physical aspect). What details about you do you want people to remember and pass along (Story aspect)? How can you motivate people to talk (Motivation aspect) and, finally, how will you make it easier for people to pass information along to others (Viral factor)? We discuss these four aspects at greater length in section I.

Physical aspect: 'Story WOM' is most effective in a one-on-one setting. Usually, face-to-face works best, but a phone conversation can have the same effect. In fact, an inherent advantage of small businesses is that, in many cases, they have an up-close-and-personal relationship with clients. Unlike corporations, they don't communicate through creative work put out by the brand department or semi-scripted call center representatives. This makes sharing 'Story WOM' much more effective.

Story aspect: To summarize the earlier parts of this chapter: The story needs to capture people's imaginations by being both memorable and repeatable. Remember, the goal of the story is not necessarily to lead directly to new sales. Creating basic awareness of your business is a great outcome, too. When people are aware of your business, and you are more memorable by way of an interesting story they have heard about you, they are more likely to think of you when they are shopping for something new.

Motivation aspect: The story we are talking about here is not about your product or service (next chapter), but more about you. I believe that, to motivate people to talk, your 'news' needs to make them feel *special*. Your story should admit them into some exclusive 'in the know' group. This feeling of exclusivity ("not a lot of people know what I know") explains why we want to hear the news first. It is also why we crave gossip. The exclusivity of knowledge is what creates the sometimes uncontrollable urge to tell more people what we've learned. Businesses can harness this basic human inclination to their advantage.

Viral aspect: For the story to be easily shareable, it needs to be newsy and conversation worthy. As we mentioned before, it also needs to be brief. Short and memorable, that's all there is to it. When the timing is right, you want people to remember you and your story, and pass it on.

Availability

When someone hears a story about you and wants to follow up, finding you should be easy. I explore this in greater depth in the 'Availability' chapter, but here are some quick tips that are relevant to 'Story WOM':

- Make it easy to search for you with easy to remember
  - ▸ Business name

- ▸ Web address
- ▸ Phone number
- ▸ Prominent sign
- Have contact information in all promotional materials that may be passed around
  - ▸ Freebies
  - ▸ Emails

Measurement and Conversion

Your goal is to find out if your story a) is passed forward (One WOM wave, or two), b) has a positive effect on the listener and, most importantly, c) converts to new sales or increased loyalty. Corporations dedicate big budgets to surveying what people say and hear, gauging their attitudes towards the WOM message and, ultimately, their actions. Smaller businesses have to go anecdotal. There are two key questions you should ask when evaluating your WOM marketing effort:

① How did you hear about me/us?

② What did you hear about me/us?

Your relationship with those you ask will affect the answers you get. Non-customers who seek information about you might be more comfortable to answer just the first question. As you develop a more substantial relationship, people will be more open about addressing the second one. Read more about this topic in the 'Measurement' Chapter.

It's hard to say resolutely that the story tactic is working. You may get some hints or anecdotes, but to undo the cause and effect of factors that lead to new business relationships is hard. In marketing, we call this the 'wild' card. Marketers often struggle with marketing efforts that are not measurable, but they still use them. For example, TV ads usually do not solicit a direct response, but can build awareness. Your approach to the 'Story tactic' should be similar: Find your stories, understand your segments, push your narrative and probe, but don't expect to determine exactly if it worked.

Chapter Summary – *What you need to know*

☑ People are probably more likely to talk about the story behind the company than about what the company makes or does.

☑ Stories need to capture the imagination and be short and memorable; think of an anecdote or "sound byte" others can repeat in about 30 seconds.

☑ Businesses can develop several stories they want to "push" depending on the segment; they can use their personal stories or those from their business.

☑ People are more likely to repeat the stories they hear from you if they:

- *Empathize with the story.*
- *Believe that your story admits them to some exclusive 'in the know' group.*
- *Story is 'juicy' or newsworthy.*

☑ The success of Story WOM can be measured by asking new customers several simple questions (see exercises below).

☑ Most important thing: Don't be shy about telling your stories. Encourage employees to tell the story as well. Make it a habit.

Exercises

☑ Try to ask customers what stories they heard about you before they knew you. (Are these positive stories? Did they have positive outcomes like new prospects calling you? Can you add some color to the story and re-introduce it to get more WOM?)

☑ Come up with two stories you believe people will pass around:
- *Think about who you can tell your stories to.*
- *What would be their motivation to tell others?*
- *When can you tell this story and how can you make a habit of it?*

☑ Rent the movie 'Gossip': A story of three college students who decide to spread a rumor. The rumor is false and malicious, but the general idea is relevant (and it's a decent thriller).

The Big Idea

As we discussed in the last chapter, crafting your story is your first WOM marketing step. Next up: Make sure that what you actually do in your business and how you go about doing it is also conversation worthy. In every city, there are scores of hairdressers, mechanics, or lawyers. Why are some more talked about than others? What can they do to heighten interest in their businesses? Ideas include supplying a product nobody else has, making a special effort in customer service, or focusing on the special needs of certain groups or individuals. Even the design of a store or the impact of a display can set a business apart. I guarantee that there is something unique about your business, or that you can create something. Once identified, you need to focus on communicating that quality to others.

Building WOM into your business routine and articulating your own personal story are the first steps to creating Natural WOM for your business. Getting people to talk about your product or service is a major accomplishment. The message can be communicated even further through Amplified WOM (which we will begin to cover in the next chapter). Achieving Natural WOM is a prerequisite for most other Amplified WOM tactics.

To be clear, WOM worthiness should not be confused with having a competitive advantage. Your business might differ from others, but that difference alone might not constitute a topic of conversation. For example, in the field of product development, not all enhancements are created equal. Case in point: will people talk about a low APR credit card or getting more minutes on their cell phones? They might, but that makes for some pretty lame conversation. People are more likely to talk about the rewards their card offers ("I was able to fly to Hawaii for free"), or to show off the ultra-slim phone they recently purchased. The latter are WOM worthy, even though the former might be considered a competitive advantage.

What Big Corporations Do

Historically, there have been three major phases in corporate product development and customer experience improvement. In the first phase (and I simplify), companies focused on the basics. Soap should clean, TVs need to transmit. When something breaks, customers require service.

As competition increased and affluence grew, a second phase emerged. Companies began coming up with unique selling points to differentiate their product or service. Customers demanded more than the basics and were able to afford it. They also had more companies to choose from. To respond to these pressures, companies began investing heavily in product development and creative advertising. Brands and brand identities became a major focus. Customization and segmentation strategies offered customers various plans and options to choose from. At the same time, companies began to look closely at the costs of a great customer experience (shopping process or servicing clients). That, coupled with the effects of competition, led to waves of re-engineering, downsizing, automating and outsourcing.

Some enlightened companies are now entering into a third phase. Businesses are beginning to take note of the effect their actions have on what customers and non customers *say* about them. For example, outsourcing a business function (call center, production) might reduce costs, but harm quality. In the second phase, companies tried to estimate the effect of outsourcing on the number of customers they could attract or maintain. In the third phase – which is WOM focused – companies expand their investigation to include what customers or non customers say about things like an outsourced call center. Negative comments can influence customer behavior. For example, they might decide to switch to a company they believe has better customer service. In essence, a company's actions have an impact not only on their direct customers, but contribute to its broader reputation. WOM about certain business practices can snowball and have a direct (though, not easily predictable) effect on the bottom line.

Positive examples of this phenomenon are high-end items in catalogues. Several companies that sell through catalogues discovered that including extravagant, expensive, over-the-top items (like a diamond covered iPod case) increases overall sales, even if nobody actually buys the wackier products. The reason for this, of course, is that those receiving the catalogue now have a reason to begin a conversation about it.

Three Phases of Corporate Marketing Focus

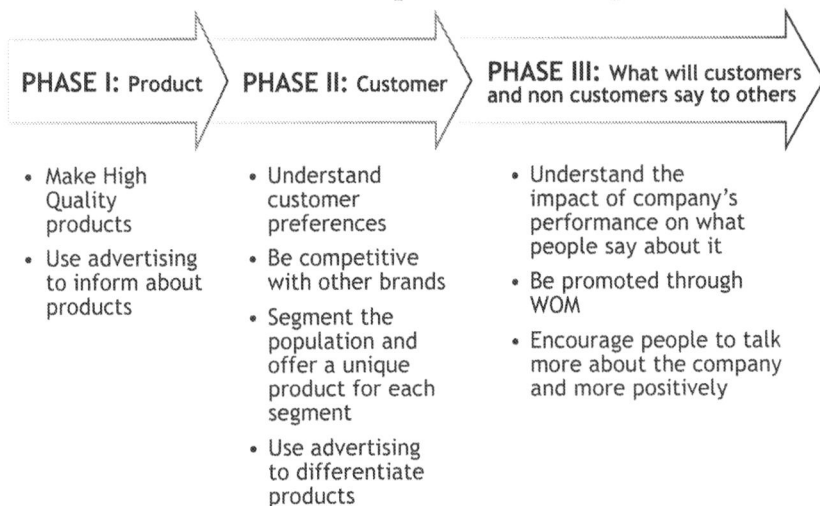

PHASE I: Product	PHASE II: Customer	PHASE III: What will customers and non customers say to others
• Make High Quality products • Use advertising to inform about products	• Understand customer preferences • Be competitive with other brands • Segment the population and offer a unique product for each segment • Use advertising to differentiate products	• Understand the impact of company's performance on what people say about it • Be promoted through WOM • Encourage people to talk more about the company and more positively

Making It Happen

Part I: Find Ideas

Building WOM into your business plan means doing something that is extraordinary, astonishing, or, at the very least, different enough to stimulate a positive conversation about you. It would be impossible to list all the ways to build WOM into your business. My aim is to stimulate your imagination and provide a framework in which you can think about your business in a WOM-worthy way. Some ideas might be bold and translate into significant changes to your business model or products. Others will be fairly simple to implement, but still have an impact on the volume and tone of WOM.

The "cool" factor: Wow = WOM

I submit that every business has or can develop something "cool" about it. I use the term "cool" very seriously in this context: It is the basic starting point for positive product conversations.

Firstly, I believe that opening and owning a small business is cool in and of itself. In other words, you don't need to look very far for your first story idea. Your experience striking out on your own can and should be told in an interesting way. I find that many entrepreneurs don't talk openly about their business. Even people in their closest circles don't know exactly what they do. That has to change in order for small business to take advantage of their relationships and get their friends and family supporting them. I am not suggesting that business owners should talk endlessly about themselves at every opportunity. I do, however, think that they should do a lot more talking.

How you talk about your business is going to determine whether the message will continue to be passed along. Your story needs to be brief, clear and memorable, and have a hook. You might have to think about this for a while. Corporations spend months refining their 'identity'.

Going back to our WOM framework, you will need to think about the various segments you interact with and tailor your story to each one. Think about which version of the story is most likely going to be repeated by a customer versus a non customer, a Neutral versus a Promoter. There is no science to this. The goal of this exercise is to think about what you can say that is most likely going to be passed along.

Secondly, you must identify something cool about what you do or the way you do it. Having a competitive advantage of some sort is a great start. I am sure you've already thought about what is better and different about your business as compared with others. As I mentioned before, a competitive advantage is not a WOM guarantee. For example, you may be able deliver a solution/product three days faster than your closet competitor, and let's say that customers know this and appreciate it. Will they talk about it to others? It's hard to say. It isn't likely to be a conversation starter, but more of an add-on to a conversation already in progress. But what would happen if the solution/product was delivered three days *before* the commitment day (even if the supplier knew they could do it early), and there was something about the delivery that was both exciting and surprising? Customers might appreciate many enhancements in the purchasing process: Extra functionality or a service that was not expected, a free coupon for next time, a free service offer, a refer-a-friend gift offer, and so on. With the Wow/cool factor is in place, WOM is much more likely to happen.

Below is a conversation-worthy starter guide loosely based on the seven Ps (formerly known as the four Ps framework). The bottom line is this: Don't follow the crowds. Think about your business, get creative and be inspired to be WOMable!

7 P'S CONVERSATION-WORTHY IDEA STARTER GUIDE

Product	
Tactic	**Example: What would people say**
Customizing your offering to each client or segment of clients in some way to make people feel "special", "acknowledged" or "unique".	I actually keep my coffee mug at that coffee shop. They have this stand where I put it after I am done. No need for a paper cup and my cup is nice and big...
Identify a need or problem from your clients or prospective clients and solve it in an unusual way.	I was pretty nervous about buying it, but they gave me the numbers of some people who are actually using it now.
Offer something nobody else is offering that is...exciting	A child in my daughter's elementary school class had a birthday party at one of those indoor playgrounds. They had some games and attractions for the adults too. It was the first time I wasn't bored at a kids' parties.
Presenting your past successes.	This landscaper took me on tour all over town to see the projects she has done.
Keep it real. Create a version that only performs the basic function – no unnecessary complications.	I loved that restaurant; it only had five items on the menu and they were all very good.
Product coolness can be seen.	Yes, I got that purse online. Who knew they could make purses from license plates?

Price	
Tactic	**Example: What would people say**
For price itself to be WOM-worthy, it must be extreme: Either high or low. I would argue that high-priced (not overpriced) products are more likely to introduce WOM than low prices. Price can create the perception of prestige or better quality.	I had to choose between two colleges for an IT course. One was a lot more expensive, but I decided it was worth it.
The way you structure pricing might be a topic of conversion.	This shop offers: 'Rent a wedding gown and get the second one free (for your friend...)'. Are you in?

Placement	
Tactic	Example: What would people say
How you place or deliver your product or service to clients can be a conversion starter.	When I opened up the box, I thought that the packing was really cool. I had to order a few more as gifts just because of that.
Location: Is the location of your business special? Is there something special in your office? Is your store design unique? Are your products available only at certain exclusive locations?	She has the first original widgets in her office. I think she got them on eBay.
Timing: Are you extremely fast? Or, on the contrary, are you admired for working diligently and thoroughly to get the job done? Alternatively, do people have to wait their turn to receive your services?	This designer told me that she is really busy in the next month or so; then she called and said that something got cancelled and she can squeeze me in. I couldn't believe it.
Packaging: Is there something special about the way that you deliver results or reports? Do your reports have more information or look professional? For a physical product, is there something about the packaging itself that is unique?	She was able to explain a whole conference in three slides. She really knew her stuff.
Service: See next section for 'Wow' moment in customer service	

Promotion	
Tactic	Example: What would people say
Any Marketing activity can lead to WOM.	I saw a sign that they are going to open a German bakery in our neighborhood. What's a German bakery?
	Their newspaper ad said that they will have Greyhound adoption this weekend only at their downtown location.
	Their website contains everything you need to know about ...

People	
Tactic	**Example: What would people say**
You and your employees are a relevant topic of conversion.	Everybody who works at the travel agency has traveled quite a bit. Photos of employees on trips are all over the office walls.
How well you present yourself: Overall professionalism, ability to build trust and credibility, even how you dress.	The guy at the Surf Shop was dressed like a 'Surfer Dude', but he gave me and the kids a lecture about water safety we will never forget.
Communication style: Will you instill confidence in your abilities, do you do an especially good job at listening to concerns and explaining options?	We told him about all the problems we had in the past with maintenance. He listened, took notes, and then explained to us that achieving what we wanted to achieve would actually cost us more than we had originally anticipated.
Employees: Their training, professionalism, dress and overall appearance. Are they motivated and helpful? Are they in a good mood?	I just love hanging out at their shop. The people there are so upbeat. I leave in a good mood.
Many businesses have very close interactions with clients and other business partners (e. g. suppliers).	I talk to her almost every week. She has my mobile number and I have hers. It's that kind of relationship.
Even in businesses that are online-only, the people who operate the business are very important. They still interact via email or phone with the outside world.	I bought this Scottish quilt from a website of a company in New England. I couldn't believe it when they called to ask if I wanted to have my name embroidered on it free of charge. The woman was so nice.

Process	
Tactic	**Example: What would people say**
Worry free: Do you make sure that people feel that you take care of all the details?	This bridal shop knows how stressed we are. They offered a last-minute dress change from their current stock. I actually used it!
Ease: Is it easy to buy from you? Is it easy to get service from you? The key is to identify the common concerns people have about purchasing from you, or the concerns that they have about your services. Then, address those concerns both in what you communicate and what you actually deliver.	The agreement is really long but he took the time to explain to me all the details about what I am actually about to sign. That made me feel so much more in control.
	The instructors in this school are committed to answering emails within 48 hours, even after the course is done. No need for office hours!

Physical Evidence/Sampling	
Tactic	**Example: What would people say**
Many products and services cannot be tangibly experienced before a purchase decision is made. For example, there is no way to try out consulting services or window replacements, as opposed to demo software. Potential customers will be more likely to buy if there is some evidence a product or service is great. Businesses usually solve this problem with references, testimonials, case studies, or press articles about their success.	He offered us a long list of references to call. It was impressive. We made a few phone calls and he came out alright.
	Her business has this online 'guestbook' where customers can record their opinions about their experiences. Not everything was positive, but most people were pretty happy.
	I read their case study on how they helped one of our competitors. You should check it out on their website.

'Wow' moment in customer service:

Customer service is a vital concept; I wanted to give it a section all its own.

After people call to learn more about your business, some will decide to buy your product or service. They then become your clients. In every interaction, you try to provide a consistently high level of customer service. That's what people expect. However, to achieve WOM, you must find ways to surprise, to go above and beyond expectations. In other words, you are looking for peak 'Wow' moments. Customers who experience these moments will be more loyal for sure, but they are also more likely to talk about their experience with others, creating WOM marketing.

Some simple examples:
- Making an extra call, visit or email that was not expected.
- Reward your customers – it's not just for credit cards. I am not talking about a coffee punch card, either. The surprise factor must be there.
- Giving something for nothing ("compliments of the chef").
- Fixing a problem quickly and giving the person some compensation ("And here's a gift card for all the trouble").
- Taking a real interest in other people (more than a hollow "how are you?").
- Be extremely (yet strategically) open about your business (options, pros and cons, you versus competitors, and so on) in the consideration/purchase phase.

The need to create a "Wow" moment in commerce is so strong that some companies create fake 'problems' for their customers (e.g. adding a change to their invoice), notify them of it, then very quickly remedy the situation. Sounds far fetched? It's out there (though highly unethical and unadvisable), and it is very likely to make people talk about it.

Prioritize and don't try to do everything. Be selective and incorporate ideas into your business routine.

Part II: Implement Ideas
Customer Touch Points

The 7 P's framework will help flesh out a variety of ideas about what makes your business unique or "cool", and, therefore, worthy of WOM. When you build WOM into your business, you will create Natural WOM. Natural WOM should be the result of the normal course of business. When you continuously interact with people, they learn something about your story or about what makes you unique. Ideally, this will encourage them talk about you.

Each customer contact creates an opportunity for you to provide them with information, or to act in a way that will make them want to talk about you positively. Marketers call these interactions Customer Touch Points. This is a really useful concept. Analyze the kinds of contact you have with people (a person doing product research visits your website, a customer calls with a question, a non customer emails a request for more information, and so on) and decide on your communications strategy. From a WOM perspective, your focus is on maximizing the number of people who talk about you post their interaction with you. The call to action is clear: You must seek to create a customer experience that makes people feel like they can't wait to tell their friends about you.

Overall, marketers think about four broad phases where you interact with customers: **Awareness**, **Consideration**, **Purchase** and **Loyalty**. At every phase, people may act because they **received** WOM about you. Similarly, every interaction with your business can also encourage them to **generate** WOM.

1. **Awareness**: Before anybody can consider your company and make a purchase, they first need to know that you exist. Awareness building focuses on making sure that you are top of mind when somebody decides to start shopping.

    Receivers of WOM: When somebody hears about your company in a casual conversation (WOM), you achieve some of level of awareness impact. The problem is that consumers are constantly bombarded with information about companies (e.g. ads) intent on achieving that same goal. Advertising is a multi-billion-dollar industry. The challenge for advertisers is to cut through the clutter to be memorable. The advantage of WOM marketing is that it is usually based on something unique enough to be conversation worthy. Awareness is more easily achieved with WOM than any other form of mass media.

    Generations of WOM: Learning about a company that does something unique may very well be a conversation starter. Once someone is aware of a new company, they then must decide if the information is "cool" enough to pass along. It is human nature to want to share interesting discoveries with others. In other words, WOM does not necessarily start with customers, or even people in the market for your product; it can happen even at an early stage of awareness.

2. **Consideration**: Whether making an impulse buy or a carefully planned purchase, customers generally weigh their options. In common parlance, we call this "shopping".

    Receivers of WOM: When a person is shopping, they seek out information from various sources. They ask advice from their personal network of friends and family. They might do some research online and read what others are thinking about your product or service. Information online can appear in Blogs, basic websites, message boards, comments in response to an article or review, and so on. As consumers ready themselves to purchase, they may contact you to hear about what you can do for them, either over the phone, or by checking out your yellow page ad or website. When potential customers reach out to you, they present an opportunity for WOM. The source is biased to be sure, but smart sales people try to give an honest picture of what they can provide and feel comfortable talking about various options. You should strive to be more of an advisor than a salesperson, positioning yourself as a trusted WOM generator rather than a commercial.

    Generators of WOM: Shopping for something can be an exciting adventure ("now that I saved for my new canoe, should I get a red one or a blue one?"). It can also be nerve wracking ("I contacted three companies to do my public relations. How do I know which one to chose?"). Shopping decisions, like any other decision, elicit various emotions. And people like to talk about them. The result: WOM in the consideration phase is continually being created. When someone is shopping and considers your product or service, what they say to others about their interaction with you can be as important as if they actually buy. Think about that for a minute. A "wow" moment, even if somebody is not and will never be your customer, can still be instrumental to the development of your business.

3. **Purchase:** The consideration phase is over; you decided what you are going to buy. There are several routes to choose from: Get a quote, decide on the best vendor or shop, and evaluate options or add-ons. If someone has already decided to buy your product or service, what steps do they need to take? Your goal in the purchase phase is to maintain a high conversion rate. Of those who consider purchasing from you, what percentage actually does?

   Receivers of WOM: When people are in the process of buying, they may solicit last-minute advice from others. Positive WOM can help seal the deal. In reality, the importance of WOM diminishes the closer a person gets to buying the product or service. At the same time, it becomes increasingly important to focus on the kind of WOM the customer will generate post-purchase.

   Generators of WOM: Just like a first date, the shopping experience is a one-time event where the seller tries to show themselves in the best possible light and the buyer nervously evaluates a potential new partner. As a seller, you can employ several methods to decrease tension and position your company as an excellent companion: Making purchasing easy, being clear and upfront about details, addressing every concern, or explaining next steps. Even so, doing all these things might still not be enough to generate WOM. You must exceed expectations, surprising or delighting your potential customers. You have to create what the customer will experience as a "wow" moment.

4. **Loyalty:** A customer is born. They experience a product or service and develop an opinion about it. Will they recommend it to others? And if so, what will they say?

   Generators of WOM: When people think about WOM marketing, they usually think about customers as key WOM generators. True enough; but they are not the only potential sources. We have already established that other phases (especially the early phases of awareness and consideration) are also very important to WOM generation. This means that creating a "wow" experience in *all* of these phases is a viable WOM marketing approach. Also, it makes sense to argue that when you use a product and hear how happy others are with it, your loyalty will increase.

   Receivers of WOM: Savvy advertisers know that commercials can help boost loyalty among those who have already purchased a product. Think about the last time you saw an ad for *your* car. How did you feel when you saw it in all its glory? The same follows for current customers who hear WOM. When they hear that others are also pleased with a product they are invested in, it helps cement their relationship with that company. It also makes them more likely to become generators of WOM, and so the cycle continues.

Your Framework for A Customer-Touch-Point Action Plan

The overarching goal of building WOM into your business is to make people aware of what is unique about you and to talk positively about you to others. Still, one size does not fit all. The message you use while networking with potential customers will differ from the one you use with current clients. You will also use a variety of approaches: Face-to-face conversations, phone, email, brochure, website, Blogs, and so on.

This sounds like a lot of work, but in reality, *you are probably already doing it.* I'm simply suggesting that you structure your thinking using a WOM marketing framework. For example, when you describe your business to a prospective customer for the first time, you probably already have a fairly well-defined pitch. Similarly, when you finish a job or sell a product, you likely engage in some conversation with the customer. To be effective, you must ask yourself how you can take advantage of these interactions to generate WOM. Once you identify your strategies, integrating them into your business operation is very important. You and your employees must have a clear understanding that for each kind of interaction, a certain kind of WOM-generating story or effort should be delivered.

For Example:

When new prospects inquire…

- Prospects can call, email, visit your website or meet you in person.
- What message or story will encourage them to talk about you in every one of these channels?
- How do you follow up on customer inquires? Do you call, email or create a pop-up window when they leave your site? Apart from providing a great customer experience, what will you communicate about your business to generate WOM?

Similarly, think about how and what to communicate to generate WOM when:

- A customer is in the process of purchasing something from you…
- As the work progresses…
- Immediately after the sale…
- Follow-up customer service…

At some point, you may find it useful to write a holistic plan detailing how to use the WOM you have built into your business in your Customer Touch Point communication strategy. If you have a few minutes, try to jot down a couple of ideas. Nothing fancy. Get a piece of paper, open an Excel or Word document and copy the headers that appear in the *table* below. Then brainstorm. After a few revisions and careful thought, you will develop a clear action plan of how to generate WOM for your business at key interaction points.

Customer Touch Point	Segment/Phase	Action/Story/message that can generate WOM
When a customer calls with a question...	Customer	We have just started offering a new product that is exciting because...
....		

Facilitate WOM about your story

Once your target audience has been exposed to your stories, your next challenge is to motivate them and facilitate information sharing (WOM). The easier it is to share, the more likely they are to do it.

In 'Your story, your first step' chapter, we mentioned several ways you can make it easier for people to share your stories:

①   Tell a unique, conversation-worthy story.

②   Make it short and memorable.

③   Use your story to build closer one-on-one relationships.

④   Make people feel "special" when they hear the story, so that in the retelling, they feel plugged in.

⑤   Give them a sense that you are sharing something that not many people know. In other words, set them up to gossip about you.

We need to expand on these basic rules as we begin to think about making it easy to WOM about your business outside of the realm of one-on-one conversations.

We will draw on the four aspects of the WOM-facilitating framework we created in the first section of the book: Physical aspect, Story aspect, Motivation aspect and Viral aspect. Let's examine several Customer Touch Points to get you started thinking about Facilitating WOM:

Promotional materials:
Freebies:

Physical aspect: Some businesses give customers or prospective customers fridge magnets, business cards, paper pads, small advice booklets, videos, and so on. These Freebies act as reminders of your business to others.

Story aspect: From a story WOM angle, you want Freebies to remind people about your unique story so that they will repeat it more often. To do that, a "story reminder" should be prominently displayed in the Freebie. For example, imagine that you are a landscaper and your claim to fame is blueprints you create before beginning a project to show prospective buyers what the final design will look like. Your Freebie can say something like, "The project comes alive before we break ground."

Motivation aspect: The idea is that when people refer to you, they have a 'talking point' about you. And not just any talking point. By design – your WOM-marketing design – what they talk about is something unique, and even "cool". It makes you look better; but more importantly, it makes them look smarter and more knowledgeable, which is very helpful in motivating them to begin talking about you.

Viral aspect: What would make it easier for people to pass information about you along? The first thing is the story itself. As we mentioned, a story is more likely to be passed along if it is a memorable (short) story. A second opportunity is created when the people you interact with share your Freebies (which reinforce your story) with others. For example, your goal might be to give a customer more than one Freebie and encourage that person to pass them along. It is imperative to ensure that there is something about the Freebie that makes it relevant mostly to your target group. For example, (continuing with the landscaper example) if your Freebie is a booklet with tips on maintaining a perfect lawn, how about giving one person multiple booklets to share with friends? Information is a great conversation starter. If the Freebie is cheap (like business cards or magnets), cost isn't a big concern. Simply ask people if they are willing to take a few and pass them along. What's the worst that could happen?

Brochures:

The Story, Motivation and Viral aspects are very similar to Freebies. The Physical aspect, however, is different:

Physical aspect: Brochures allow significantly more space than Freebies to both describe your product and push your story. But keep it simple; identify the one or two unique things you want people to talk about, and make them prominent. Some of the most successful creative executions I have seen include lots of 'white space' (blank space).

Email:

Many businesses use email to communicate with customers. Broadly speaking, there are two kinds of email communications: Broadcast email (sent to a group of people or an automated email) and person-to-person email (customized email similar to what you would send to a friend). Emails are one of the most efficient vehicles to facilitate WOM. What could be easier than press forward and pass information along?

📖 Read about all aspects of Email WOM in the Viral Marketing Chapter.

Website:

Physical aspect: Many businesses have a website, and today it is fairly easy and inexpensive to maintain one. A business website usually has three main objectives:

① To sell something directly from the site.

② Online storefront: If somebody is looking for a cake decorator, the website provides information about how to contact the company.

③ Information sharing: A website can link to articles and other resources about issues relevant to the company's offering. The website can also have unique content, like a Blog detailing the owner's thoughts or message boards, RSS feeds, and so on.

Story aspect: All the aforementioned promotional materials can communicate something about your business that is interesting enough to deserve WOM. We focused on the first two in this chapter and the one preceding it. We go deeper into how Information Sharing on your website can, by itself, generate WOM in the 'Information Sharing and Product Experience' Chapter.

Viral aspect: Your goal is to ensure that prospective customers find your website and pass it along. Another aim might be to get people to email links to their friends, or even link their site to yours (this is a side benefit to your Search Engine Optimization efforts). An online presence can facilitate WOM (make it easy to pass to others). People used to refer to the Yellow Pages when searching for a product or service provider. Today, websites are not only easier to share between friends; they are a lot more creative and provide more information than Yellow Page ads. Use them to your advantage.

A couple of basic tactics to help facilitate website-based WOM:

① A 'Refer a friend' or 'Share this with others' button in various parts of your website is very effective.

② An easy-to-remember web address can help facilitate offline conversations. If somebody is talking about you and can recall your web address, it is much easier for the listener to follow up.

Motivation aspect: Design a clear call to action – tell people why they should forward the information to others. I see many websites that say "and don't forget to tell all your friends", but fail to make a case for why should I bother. WOM is similar to every other marketing effort in this way: Your business needs a thoughtful, well-presented sales pitch. Try to answer two basic questions for the potential forwarder: What's in it for me and what's in it for the person I am forwarding this to?

One-on-one conversations (face-to-face, phone):

The concept of facilitating WOM by building it into your business is similar to the 'Story WOM' approach (Chapter 7). However, there are some key differences that deserve attention.

Physical aspect: Unlike a 'WOM Story', more business-related stories or experiences are dependent on the timing of the interaction and the segment the customer belongs to. For example, your approach to each conversation will change dramatically between the awareness, consideration or purchase phases. It also matters if you perceive the person to be a Promoter or just Neutral. Clearly, if a person is in one of the extreme segments (Hostile or Evangelist), your approach will change as well.

When thinking about how to converse with different segments, here are a couple of options to think about:

① You decide to engage in a conversation to generate WOM. Is the timing right?

② Using the appropriate tone can put listeners in the right set of mind to facilitate WOM. Plus, the right tone in the right circumstances might be worth a WOM conversation by itself: The idea is that tone that is somewhat out of the ordinary can be different enough to be memorable and worth a later conversation. For example:

- Excited ➲ about what you can and have achieved for your clients.
- Conciliatory ➲ if a bad experience occurred, you can turn it around.
- Aloof ➲ avoid over selling.
- Open ➲ willing to discuss options.
- Concerned ➲ ready to share advice.
- Urgent ➲ "There is such high demand. This week is really busy. I can squeeze you in next week."

③ The amount of information you feel the listener can comfortably absorb and potentially pass on.

Story aspect: Decide what to hype with each segment at each of the Customer Touch Point phases. In other words, when somebody calls or you meet someone, you should have a menu of options to choose from. Which aspect of your business would you like to highlight? The question you need to ask yourself is: Given the phase the client is in (awareness, consideration, and so on) and their segment (non customer, Neutral), what can I share with them that is the most likely to be passed on?

Motivation aspect: In the 'Story WOM' section, we talked about how people feel "special" when they have been given exclusive access to information, and they are more motivated to share that information with others. This human characteristic should be taken advantage of in the context of this chapter as well. Think of ways to communicate the message, "I have a special offer for a limited time", in a way that sounds genuine. Again, this is one of the significant advantages small businesses have. Your closer personal relationships with customers, and even non customers, means that you will be able to pull this marketing approach off.

More broadly, when you communicate that there is something unique and conversation-worthy about your business, or that you have something special going on right now, you create excitement. Its like finding a steal of a deal in a flea market: You can't wait to take it home, and to tell others about how cool you are for scooping it up before someone else did. Unlike a flea market, when people talk about the new company they have discovered (and how unique it is), listeners can go and get exactly the same thing.

Viral aspect: As I've said before, 'Story WOM' needs to be brief and memorable. We can all relate to the trials and tribulations of starting a business from scratch; but when you are trying to spur on conversations about what you do and how you do it, relevancy becomes important. What's unique about your business must relate to the purchasing decisions of current and prospective clients. For example, if you tell a customer about your cool new product, you hope that the information will be relevant to someone else and, thus, worth a future conversation. When a customer relates to a story, they will be able to think of at least one more person who will be interested in it as well, creating the potential for a WOM conversation.

Availability, Measurement and conversion

Making sure that you are easy to find (availability), measuring results and working towards converting WOM conversations into more business are the concepts that close the loop in every marketing effort. Chapters in this book address these topics, and I encourage you to review them before launching your WOM efforts. At the very least, read about them in Section I at the beginning of the book.

Transition to Amplified WOM

The last few chapters focused on how, in the normal course of business, you can try to encourage more people to talk about you more positively to more people (Natural WOM). The remainder of the book will focus on deliberate tactics you can use to encourage people to generate WOM (Amplified WOM). Providing customers with good reasons to do Natural WOM forms the best basis for an Amplified WOM campaign. It is hard to amplify something that doesn't exist.

Chapter Summary – *What you need to know*

☑ What you do and how you do it can be conversation worthy.

☑ Building WOM into your business is a different concept than creating a competitive advantage; a competitive advantage, for example lower price, can be too mundane to spark further conversations.

☑ Being "cool" in some way is a concept WOM marketers take very seriously: It is the basic starting point for positive product conversations.

☑ Businesses can use the 7 P's Conversation-Worthy Idea Starter Guide to brainstorm ideas.

☑ A 'Wow' moment in customer service is an especially powerful WOM igniter.

☑ A great goal to have is that at every stage of the purchasing cycle (awareness, consideration, purchase and loyalty), people will be receiving WOM about you that drives them to the next step and that, at the same time, they will generate WOM about how cool their experience with you has been.

☑ It is important to have a deliberate plan on how to motivate people to talk about you to others (facilitate WOM). In the next chapters, we go through ideas on how to achieve this through conversations, promotional materials, websites, and so on.

Exercises

☑ Use the 7 P's framework to begin developing ideas for stories for your business. Do some of the brainstorming yourself, but ask others to go through the exercise as well.

☑ Create a plan for every kind of customer interaction (new prospect calls, service email, etc) on what story are you going to "push" (see table in the chapter).

☑ From the list of ideas in the 'Facilitate WOM' section, think of two things you can do in the short term.

☑ Overall, pay more attention to conversations you are having with others on products. Notice how others tell a story about products or companies they use. What did they consider conversation worthy? Would you repeat these stories to others? Why or why not?

9 TWO-WAY CONVERSATIONS

The Big Idea

In running your business, every interaction you have with customers, information seekers or even suppliers is a chance to promote your business and generate WOM. A Two-way conversation (TWC) involves the following components:

- Asking for feedback (on your work, on the experience of buying from you, and so on).
- Listening to the feedback, ask questions to clarify.
- Following up with action or make a commitment to improve practices.
- Proactively asking your listener to generate WOM.
- Giving them something (story, email or physical) to pass along.

TWC has three major goals:

① To learn something from the conversation and improve.
② To make customers aware of your business and your genuine efforts to improve it so that they will be more willing to recommend you to others.
③ To create the opportunity to ask for WOM.

TWC is not just about ensuring customer satisfaction. It is also about developing a deeper, more personal connection with your customer. When you ask somebody to give you advice or feedback, they have to put themselves in your shoes. TWC itself may be a topic of conversation ("It was great because, before the crew left, they asked me what was good and what needed improvement."). More importantly, TWC is a breeding ground for WOM because it engages both parties in a relationship. After a TWC, people are more likely to participate in whatever WOM marketing you employ (your story, built in WOM, pass-alongs). If you ask them directly for WOM, they are more likely to follow up.

What Big Corporations Do

Big businesses make major investments in market research aimed at unearthing consumer attitudes. They undertake surveys and pulse checks. They perform focus groups and one-on-one interviews. They listen to customer service calls and reply to customer complaints. They closely observe trends in customer behavior or purchasing rates.

None of these methods equals a Two-way conversation.

A corporation can approximate a TWC when they ask a customer for their opinion and act on it. As is true for any relationship, people invest more in those who demonstrate concern or interest in them. In commerce, that translates into patronage and positive WOM.

Some enlightened companies, like Intuit (QuickBooks), try to listen and react to customer feedback. They even publish reports about how they have altered their products or corporate practices based on feedback; but the majority of big businesses are not nimble enough to change quickly (unless they see a direct impact on their bottom line). It's hard for them to admit wrong doing, or even that some practices are flawed. That kind of confidence and openness is not common place.

Making It Happen

Segments

Regardless of who you talk to, you can always ask for opinions. Yes, we all dislike when somebody bothers us with a survey at dinnertime; but if you are talking to a customer or someone who called you with a question, it is more acceptable to ask for their thoughts.

Two-way conversation by segment:

Non Customers:

Focus on their shopping experience so far and *ask*:

- Was it easy to find you?
- How did they hear about you?
- Did they hear any feedback about you from others? Is there anything you can do better?
- Ask about their concerns or doubts. Are your products or service able to alleviate some of these? Is there anything you are not addressing?
- Ask them about their end goal in shopping (e.g. what they are going to use the product or service for, not what it is). What's exciting about it? Does what you do help them fulfill their goals?

Follow up (or at least commit to following up) on things that are unclear or need changing.

- *Try to help immediately:*
  - Help clarify issues by giving more information or explanations.
  - Add an extra site visit, product demonstration or present a project already completed.
  - Refer to somebody who is experienced with the issue at hand, either from within the company or outside of it.
- *Describe future changes:*
  - Show empathy for concerns and calls for change.
  - Mirror comments by repeating them using your own words/descriptions.
  - Explain what you *can* do given other constraints in your business, and when.
    - Show genuine resolve and commitment to making things better.
  - Explain what you *cannot* do because of various constraints.
    - Commonly, customer may say that they want long-lasting, multi-featured products, but the price is too high for them.
- *Focus on the positive, too:*
  - Listen carefully to what people like about your business. Building on your strengths is sometimes more important than fixing what's not working.
  - In my experience, if people really like a certain thing about you, they will be:
    - A lot more forgiving on other aspects.
    - WOM about the positive.

Proactively try to generate WOM

Your Two-way Conversation by itself is a WOM-generating action. Your listeners are now more involved your business and perhaps feel a higher level of ownership of its success. As a result, the likelihood of their promoting you to others is higher

Apply Natural WOM tactics:

- Your Story, your first step: near the end of a TWC is a great time to tell people your story.
- Building WOM into your business, part one: Tell them about something unique, even "cool" about your business. This might be a follow up to one of their comments, or more of an FYI.
- Building WOM into your business, part two: Share with them one of

your promotional materials (Freebies, Brochure, Email and Website) that can generate WOM.

- Ask them to WOM! They may not follow up on it, but you can always ask. Explain to them why WOMing is important to you, and how it can be beneficial or fun for others to hear. Be proactive, don't be shy.
- Make TWC and efforts to generate WOM a part of your routine. Make sure that both you and your employees continuously do it.

Customers:

Most of what appears above regarding Non Customers is applicable to Customers, but with a few additions:

Focus on customer experience:

- Ask open-ended questions about customers' experience (what worked and what needs improvement).
- Sometimes, open-ended question result in dead air, or people find it hard to engage in the conversation. In that case, try to find an aspect of your business you already know people either really like or have a problem with. Ask people's opinion about it just to get the conversation going. Remember, the goal of the conversation (from a WOM perspective) is to create instant intimacy.

Follow up (or at least commit to following up) on things that are unclear or need changing.

- Similar to Non customers; but also…
- A TWC is great opportunity to create a 'Wow' moment in customer service. Decisively and quickly following up after hearing about a customer concern is bound to generate WOM. The opposite is also true: If they were absolutely blown away by something that you did, show them how you can do more of it for them (or offer to do the same for people they know).

Proactively try to generate WOM:

Similar to Non Customers, with several notable differences:

- You may feel more comfortable asking Customers to WOM.
- Customers know more about your business and can be better ambassadors. When they WOM about you, they can answer more questions and are considered a more credible source given their relationship with you.
- While most Non Customers on the Endorsement Spectrum will be in the Neutral camp, at least some of your Customers will be Promoters or Evangelists. You should focus more effort on those groups. Being a Promoter means that a person thinks positively about your business, not necessary that he or she will actually talk about it to others. As a result, make sure that you give perceived Promoters the attention they deserve

(talk to them more, give them materials to pass along [stories, email, physical]), and, most importantly, motivate them to pass them along.

- Try to see if you can recruit them to your :
  - ‣ Reference/Recommendation Group
  - ‣ Buzz team
  - ‣ Refer-a-friend program
- Similarly, give more attention to Neutrals with a big social circle or those who possess strong tech abilities.

Finally, decide on the WOM-generating activities you should do with pretty much all of your Customers. Most of the WOM tactics I describe in the book are low cost and can be incorporated into the ongoing operation of the business.

Two- way conversation in a real-life context:

It is easy for a contractor to drive the last nail and move on to the next project; but if he wants to turn customers into repeat customers who will recommend his services to others, he must engage them in a two-way conversation. This is not just about making sure that clients are satisfied. It is about discussing what went well and not so well. Everybody is nervous about work done on their biggest investment - their house. As a result, many people are willing to do post-mortem analysis on repair jobs. Contractors can start with open-ended questions like, "How did I do? What went well and what needs improvement?" They need to show real interest, listen and take notes. Something that simple can make people feel they are not just another transaction. By asking for feedback, a service-provider is essentially saying, "I want to build my business, I want to build myself, and I want to ask for your help." Following this conversation, a contractor can share their unique story or emphasize what makes them a unique contractor. They can leave business cards or Freebies, and, most importantly, proactively ask for WOM. For example, a contractor can ask for referrals if the listener knows anyone needing home renovations.

Chapter Summary – *What you need to know*

- ☑ Two way conversations (TWC) begin by you asking for feedback on your business, listening to comments and clarifying issues raised and then promising to make things better.

- ☑ Engaging others in thinking about your businesses, your openness to listen and building a relationship create the opportunity to ask for WOM.

- ☑ Indeed, the next step in a TWC is to ask others to WOM on your behalf, then give them something to facilitate WOM (story, email, promotional material, etc).

Exercises

- ☑ Practice Two-way conversation. In the same way you prepared for job interviews in the past, think about the points you want to make in advance.

- ☑ Try a Two way conversation next time you have time to speak to a customer or anybody else that can pass WOM about you.

- ☑ After several tries at TWCs, analyze what works and what doesn't. Find more people and opportunities to carry on effective TWC.

The Big Idea

Business owners know that networking is important. Almost every business marketing guide contains a section dealing with it. Since it is something you are probably already doing, what strategies can you use to encourage the people you interact with to talk to more people and start multiple WOM waves?

The key difference between networking and networking for WOM is the balance between quality and quantity. Most guides on the subject will point out that successful networking is about building genuine relationships. Parties must have some real interest in each other and believe that they will mutually benefit from the relationship. In a nutshell, networking involves making new friends. Networking for WOM is a less involved form of networking. As you network, you will talk to many people who are not going to become contacts, friends or customers. Those conversations are not a waste of time, but a chance for you to apply the techniques contained in this book.

What Big Corporations Do

Corporations that market to consumers don't really network with them. Business-to-consumer companies (B2C) only interact indirectly using mass marketing, market research or watching online chatter. The beacon in corporate America on how to turn networking into WOM is Business-to-business (B2B) companies. These are companies that create products and services that are used in other companies' production processes. For example, a car manufacturer has to buy robots, assembly line equipment, quality assurance software and crash-test-dummies from various B2B companies.

Just like small businesses, B2B's marketing is focused on a few buyers and not on a mass market. As a result, regular advertising is fairly rare and WOM is extremely important.

B2B companies use various forms of networking-based WOM marketing:

① **Face-to-face Networking**

Popular venues are:

▸ Conferences

▸ Trade shows

▸ Industry associations

▸ Company sponsored events

▸ Topical events created by the company (like a consulting company promoting their latest book, for example Bain's "Profit from the Core", or Apple's user group meetings).

② **In-house phone, mail or email lists**

B2B companies communicate with their customers using newsletters, support centers that can answer questions, and so on. Similarly, B2Bs strive to maintain a relationship with prospective customers who have shown interest in the past. Choice of channels is dependent on the cost of the channel and importance of the person. Big fish get phone calls; smaller ones are on the email newsletter list.

③ **Influencer networking**

B2Bs try to network and develop a relationship with people who are often called upon to give their advice about companies in the field. Examples include industry analysts, university professors or reporters. Part of building this relationship involves feeding those influencers unique content that they can publish, thus helping influencers build their personal brand as experts. For similar reasons, they also offer Influencers access to people in the company who usually don't speak to the outside world.

④ **Customer Referral Programs**

B2Bs seek out satisfied customers and successful projects and present their stories. That may include testimonials (online through website, webinars, podcasts, Blogs, or offline in marketing materials like brochures or white papers). Some referral programs actually connect people (referrals) to those seeking to buy from the company.

⑤ **Cold calling**

▸ Today mostly done by email (" Hi. We attended the same conference and wanted to introduce myself…", or "I saw an article about your company and thought that our company might help in…").

▸ Not a WOM starter; more of a chance to begin some form of relationship that can later lead to WOM.

⑥ **Public relations and other advertising**

▸ Important to support other WOM campaigns. The least credible

WOM starter, but serves as a reminder of messages already out there.

The challenge that Business-to-Business companies face in networking that makes WOM important is that big-ticket purchasing decisions are often not made by the first person they meet. Many people in the organization can influence a decision. In fact, decision making is sometimes done by committee, or is influenced by consulting firms that specialize in advising on purchases.

The bottom line is that when B2B firms talk to a potential purchaser company rep, they must present their story in a way that is persuasive and memorable. They need to make it easy to pass the information along and somehow motivate the person to do so. How do smart B2Bs achieve this? They try to make their contact look smart and resourceful. Imagine that you are a manager in a big IT firm. You go to a conference and a B2B company shows you how to slash costs, give unique functionality to your unit or presents a strong case for some form of partnership. Taking the ideas back to headquarters will make you look really good, even if the ideas are not implemented. B2B marketers work hard to create ready-made presentations and talking points for those who want to sell their ideas internally. They try to show a real interest in their potential clients' strategic focus and areas of concern. They continuously offer their help as subject-matter experts. This can be done in the form of information sharing (online, e.g. webinars; or offline, e.g. white papers). Some will even do an on-site visit or a no-cost strategy discussion. To summarize, the focus is on "what can I do for you so you will pass the information along", as opposed to, "here's my sales pitch, are you or anybody else that you know interested?"

To bring all of this back to small-venture WOM marketing, just substitute the company insider in the IT firm example above with whomever you are networking with about your business. There is every reason to believe that the same principles that work for B2Bs who are trying to convert networking into WOM will work for you.

Networking also offers an opportunity to conduct market research. People have opinions about what B2B companies sell. Networking creates a forum for sharing these opinions. B2Bs can create anonymous surveys that ask potential buyers about their opinion, but those will get very low response rates and, in any case, responders don't have a good reason to be very forthcoming about their opinions. Networking allows B2B companies to hear:

- What are the top issues on peoples' minds currently?
- What do they think about the B2B company and, as importantly, its competitors?
- Commonly held views about the industry, specific products or the buying process.
- Any major reservations or fears about a new purchase.

All of those insights can be extremely valuable in shaping the way B2Bs design their product offerings and determine how to sell them. They create a starting point for companies to begin searching for the next 'big idea' in their WOM efforts.

When it comes to customers or prospects that have already shown some interest, WOM is focused on maintaining the relationship through information sharing. Many B2Bs "keep in touch" with these groups on a regular basis. For bigger clients, it can be a personal email or phone call. For smaller ones, maybe a customized email newsletter. Prospects have already opted into the company's database, saying, "keep me in the loop, I want learn more about you." To get the most attention from any communication, it is important to customize content for information needs (e.g. want to learn about latest trends versus want to hear when you have new products or specials). This kind of follow up represents not only smart 'fanning of the flames', but multiple opportunities for WOM to begin. In all those communications, B2B can push "cool" WOM-worthy information that is likely to be passed along.

Making It Happen

There is a lot to learn from how B2Bs turn networking into WOM. Their tactics can be adapted by every marketer.

Businesses, especially those that don't spend any money on advertising, know the importance of networking. There are several popular networking hubs

Small businesses are likely to use:

- Family and friends
- Religious community
- Personal or professional network
- Professional association
- Chamber of Commerce or other business clubs
- Hobbies or special interest groups
- Professional gatherings (conferences, business presentations)

When Small Business Owners attend a networking event, they should have two goals in mind: The *first* is to try to meet people who will potentially become long-term contacts or evolve into clients in the near future. Most networking professionals will attest that a two-hour networking event will usually not produce more than two good contacts, even though, you talk to more than two people at a networking event. How can you get the most out of your investment in those conversations? The answer (and *second* goal): Let people know what's unique and conversation-worthy about you or your company, and encourage your listener to WOM. Think of networking as multiple opportunities to create awareness about your work and to encourage people to talk about it.

Some basic principles in Networking for WOM:
Make others feel special – Listen First

People who speak to (skillful) politicians often report that, for at least a few minutes during the conversation, they felt like they were the center of his or her attention. A politician may ask a variety of questions that create the impression that they are genuinely interested in the other person, or that they sympathize with them. Nothing distracts them, even in a crowded room. Being part of this kind of conversation gives you a great feeling, and it certainly showcases the skills of professional networkers. They may only spend five minutes with someone, but they make that person feel like they really matter. This speedy Two-Way Conversation (TWC) can create instant intimacy that is fertile ground for WOM generation. I am not suggesting that every conversation *has* to start with you listening; but I do believe that some level of active listening needs to happen before you start working on generating WOM or asking for WOM.

Use your stories strategically – cast a wide net

You've done some active listening; now it's your turn. What you've heard will have given you some clue which story to pull out of your grab bag. Is this person in your target market? Did you get any hint as to who they can potentially influence? Answers to these kinds of questions help you customize the story accordingly; but in most cases you won't have that information. Your solution: Cast a wide net. Talk to as many people as you can, tell your most conversation-worthy stories and hope for the best WOM results.

Conversely, let's imagine that you end up talking to somebody who is motivated and able to spread the word (Influencer, knows many people, uses technology well – e.g. has a Blog). It goes without saying that you should try to spend more time with that person and ask to follow up with them later. In this case, you want to keep track of the person because of the volume of WOM they can generate, not because they create direct business.

Motivate them to WOM

Think about B2Bs that try to motivate a company insider to WOM about their new product: If we (the B2B) make the insider look good when they present our new business proposal, he or she will be motivated to go along. This thinking also holds true for small businesses. One of the reasons we talk is because we want to project a positive image of ourselves.

Supplying your listener with story material that makes them look good is your goal in a networking environment. A comic personal anecdote can help your listener sound witty when they relay it forward. Mentioning a unique business achievement that solicits a 'wow' from your listener may get a similar response when your listener tells the same story to others. Either case, they have a reason to talk.

As always with Story WOM, remember to keep them short and memorable.

Offer to be a Subject Matter Expert

One great way to guarantee a follow up call is to offer a future consultation. A contractor who offers to advise on any future problems, or a public relations professional who mentions they are willing to review a media kit and provide feedback are at least somewhat likely to get a second call. Most companies in the world would love to have the ability to offer prospective clients a 'free trail period' or a 'free assessment/quote". Positioning yourself as a Subject Matter Expert is a much more customized and personal way to achieve this. Also, don't forget to mention to your listener that they are free to offer your expertise to anyone they know. This point signals that you know how to reconcile trying to sell with actually helping someone out.

Facilitate WOM

Make it easy to follow up with you, both for your listeners and the people they talk to.

- *Ask them if they want to learn more about you:*
  - Become part of an opt-in group that receives your emails or newsletters
  - Ask for *their* business card or email
  - Follow up with an email that they can send along to others
- *Tell them about your easy-to-remember web address or phone number.*
- *Point to unique information (website, blog, newsletter) they or others can access.*
- *Make your business card WOM.*
  - A business card is the most basic thing to give out
  - One dimensional, traditional, name+address+logo cards will not lead to WOM
  - To generate WOM from your card:
    - Refer to your most conversation-worthy story
    - Point to your online presence, suggest why people should email you, or mention your 'refer-a-friend' program
    - Use the front *and* the back of the card to communicate

Follow Up – your second chance for WOM generation

You took the other person's card, or maybe they even emailed you ("it was great meeting you at the …"). This second chance to generate WOM with a person you met at the networking event will probably be more fruitful than the first. Most follow ups will happen through email, and that's great news for WOM marketing. You can create a great email (with the idea that it will be forwarded; see Viral Marketing in chapter 13). By the way, I am not suggesting that email is better than a conversation for WOM, but rather an email following a one-on-one conversation can be very effective in reminding people to WOM and making it easy for them to do so.

Market Research

When they network, B2Bs use every opportunity to gain intelligence about opinions and attitudes towards them and the market as a whole. You can, too. In fact, even in large B2C (Business-to-consumer) companies, executives sometime base their opinions of their own products on feedback they receive from a small group of personal friends or family. You are probably thinking: But the sample size is so small, why trust this type of 'market research'? There are several reasons why. First, if something is amiss with your product or website, you only need one person to notice it. Secondly, if you ask 100 people for their opinion about a product, you won't hear 100 opinions, but more likely a convergence of two or three major themes. Anecdotal evidence should be treated with caution, but feedback usually deserves some attention. Take the time to solicit your networking partners' opinions and advice. This can be done at the networking event, but can potentially be even more effective in an email exchange following the meeting.

Chapter Summary – *What you need to know*

- ☑ You are probably already doing so some form of networking currently.

- ☑ Networking usually entails creating mid to long-term relationships with new people.

- ☑ The goal of Networking for WOM is to use even brief chit-chat in a networking situation to generate WOM.

- ☑ For example, if you go to an event, you are probably not going to make more than one or two meaningful new contacts. However, you are likely to talk to many more. Those interactions and the stories you tell in them should lead to WOM generation.

- ☑ There are several best practices in networking for WOM.
  - *Find out more hubs for networking (are there groups you've heard about but never went to their meetings?)*
  - *Make others feels special by listening first.*
  - *Find a great, funny, juicy story you believe that your listener is likely to repeat.*
  - *Facilitate WOM by making sure they know how to direct people to you (name of company or website, business card, etc).*
  - *Email more information to people, even those who will never do business with you directly, but will potentially forward your 'very interesting' email to others.*
  - *Networking is also a great chance for businesses to do some market research. What you hear might be eye-opening.*

Exercises

☑ Don't wait for that next big chamber of commerce event to test your way into Networking for WOM. Instead, next time you talk to somebody you meet for the first time (and have several minutes of his/her time), try it.

- *Remember that Networking for WOM starts with you listening first, but that soon after you actively plant your story and try to facilitate WOM.*

INFORMATION SHARING AND PRODUCT EXPERIENCE FOR WOM

The Big Idea

Businesses are regularly encouraged to promote themselves by sharing information about their business, or by providing samples of their products. I enthusiastically encourage this strategy as a great way to build your business; but it is only part one of the story. Part two, involves thinking about how to motivate listeners and samplers to talk about your company to others. Information sharing and product experience teaches people something about you; how can you facilitate the transfer of that experience and knowledge to others?

There are two major groups of Information sharing and product experience: Outbound and Inbound.

Outbound:

Definition: Actively reaching out to others

Outbound information-sharing examples: Speaking engagements, article writing, newsletters (offline or online), media interviews, advertising in all its forms. Less formally: reaching out to prospective clients to talk about your business (or tell your story).

Outbound product sampling examples: Display your actual product in a public place (e.g. a supermarket tasting station, a stand in a fair, a tent in a sporting event), sales 'party' (similar to Mary Kay or Pampered Chef), and a trailer with product displays on board that reaches various towns all over the country.

Inbound:

Definition: Making knowledge available for information seekers

Inbound information sharing examples: Free consultation, free quotes, website info, Webinar, Blog, RSS feeds, Podcasts, case studies, white papers.

Inbound product sampling examples: Website info, Product demos, product sample, coupons, user stories or testimonials.

Online inbound information-sharing (Blogs, Podcasts) receive a lot of press. Is there something behind the hype? Yes, for a select few companies, like those that deal in information (consultants), or use their website as their main business driver, or companies with unique or complex products. These need more than a basic product description to make a new sale. A marketing consultant needs to do more than provide a list of the ten things she can do (direct marketing, store design, public relations, and so on). She must make people understand in detail and in *technicolor* what she can actually achieve. She also wants to inspire confidence in her abilities. She may decide to start a Blog as a forum for her unique insights. It will allow her to appear as an expert, and can function as a sort of expanded business card. If the information is relevant, people searching for info on a topic might stumble on her site. I can make a similar case as to why making case studies available about her work, or offering a free half-hour consultation might help her stand out in the crowd.

The catch for small businesses is that they generally don't possess unique knowledge or sell complex products. If that is you, then you need to be very careful about spending a lot of time on Blogging or website design. There are probably some basic principles that every small business should follow:

① Make sure that you know what people's concerns are and have a way to proactively address them. Provide that information on a website or in printed materials. Make a point of addressing issues with prospective clients (face-to-face, phone or email).

② Every person is different, so people may have unique questions or needs that you have not yet addressed. Make sure people know that you are enthusiastically available for consultation (in person or by email or phone).

③ Make learning about you cool and fun. Every business owner can answer a phone, respond to an email or create an FAQ on a website. How are you different? A friend recently told me about choosing a cleaning service for his house. Many companies offered reliable, courteous service, but one company offered (in their yellow page ad) to be there in one hour. One hour? That pitch was intriguing enough for him to give them a call.

Herein lies the WOM aspect of information sharing. Many businesses have made the mistake of thinking that a flashy website or a podcast can, in and of themselves, draw people in and even lead to WOM. The "cool" effect of technology, however, wears off very quickly; only quality content has a fighting chance of enduring. Technology is simply its enabler. A unique combination of message, approach, content and technology in information sharing is the recipe for potential WOM (various examples reviewed in the "Making it happen" section).

Being "findable" is key when it comes to online presence (e. g. when searched in Google/Yahoo/MSN or being listed on online yellow/super pages). Websites that represent businesses with mostly offline presence (from a hair salon to a plumber) must achieve some basic goals. Sites should resemble professional-looking business cards and not much more. Keep them simple, and don't waste time and effort.

Inbound product sampling is a very different story. When people agree to try your product or receive your services, you are already on your way to acquiring a new customer. Sampling is, essentially, a mini-purchase decision. They demonstrate some level of commitment to your company. While it is low risk for them, it is potentially costly for you. Considering that not every product sampler will become a customer, you should focus on, at the very least, getting them to talk about their new experience with others. The WOM effect of product sampling is often overlooked. What can you do, for example, to encourage samplers to persuade others to sample too?

Similar principles apply when people experience your company vicariously, as they do while reading case studies or testimonials (a form of inbound product sampling). Your first goal is to make third-person product experience relevant and engaging for prospective customers. Following closely should be an effort to design these pieces to appear interesting or "cool" enough that readers will want to send them along to others.

Outbound information sharing and product sampling are great ways to launch and promote a small business. Every business should benefit from aggressively trying to reach out to potential new customers and engaging in conversations with them (and encouraging them to talk to others about their experience with you). The most basic way to do that is through networking (covered in Chapter 10). There are other ways to achieve this goal that focus on getting instant access to a large crowd. For example, getting the media to report on a business or sharing your knowledge with a group of people (e. g. a lecture). Similarly, proactively getting people to experience your products and services goes a long way towards achieving both direct sales and WOM goals. Think about companies that focus on sales 'parties' in people's homes, like Amway. The ability of their motivated sales staff to gather a crowd and offer them sample products, enjoying themselves all the while, is the basis of an insanely successful business model. There are multiple WOM opportunities in outbound product sampling events that go above and beyond the product itself. For example, the invitation to the event, the event itself, the participants (who comes and what they say), samples that were given to give others, actual purchases: All of these can be designed to be conversation-worthy

What Big Corporations Do

Outbound Information Sharing

Most corporate outbound information sharing involves advertising and PR, and is very top down. They usually don't share much information about their products, or describe choices, but rather make statements that are sometimes vague and confusing. Some companies will talk more candidly in professional forums, like conventions; but I've yet to hear of a cell phone company executive giving hints on how to choose phones. Public relations can be used to remind consumers that there are people behind the brand, but large corporations use this tool sparingly.

Corporations desire to be closer and more personal with customers, but they are having a hard time fulfilling this vision. The concept of a personal advisor, banker or shopper is frequently mentioned in boardrooms, but proves too costly in practice. One-on-one communication between corporations and individuals is, at best, efficient, but usually feels far from warm and fuzzy. How do you feel when you get an email that reads, "we appreciate your business"? Much has been written about how consumers are zoning out now that they are being exposed to an overwhelming amount of mass advertising. Take television: Boston Consulting Group reports that between 1980 and 2000, the number of ads the average American TV viewer is exposed to has gone up by 75 percent. The key reason is *not* that people watch more TV, but because there are more advertising minutes per hour of broadcasting.

The small business advantage is that people relate to other human beings more than they relate to brands. These relationships and personal attachments outweigh more tangible aspects of a product offering when small and large businesses compete. People will be willing to pay more for a partnership with you. This relationship does not guarantee WOM will be generated, but experience shows that it is much more likely to.

Consider these findings: A survey by The Keller Fay Group shows that 92 percent of WOM conversations or 'Buzz' happens *offline*. Another study by Walter Carl from Northeastern University has put that figure at 80 percent.

A Sharpe Partners study revealed that 90 percent of Internet users share content via email. That's supposed to be great news for corporate marketers; alas, a closer look at *what* is being shared paints a different picture. Only 24 percent of messages are about business or personal finance. At the top of list with 88 percent are jokes and cartoons, followed by news, health care, spiritual/religious content and games (52, 32, 30, and 25 percent respectively). I bet that 100 percent of people share personal content.

The fact that people usually talk about products in person and not via email is great news for business owners. Unlike corporations, they do most of their WOM marketing in person. I don't have numbers to prove it, but I think it goes without saying that conversations are more likely than advertising to lead to more conversations. By their nature, conversations create intimacy; they facilitate the exchange of ideas with few distractions. They are the ultimate WOM marketing platform. By design, I started this book with various chapters mostly focused on conversation-based WOM marketing (Story WOM, Two-way conversation, Networking).

Outbound Product Sampling

When done well, Outbound Product Sampling can be a great way to generate WOM. I have seen several case studies of successful corporate campaigns launched this way. Here are a few examples:

- Dell Truck: Dell has limited offline presence (stores). They stocked a truck with Dell products and traveled the country, allowing people to interact with them. Events and promotions helped ensure that consumer traffic found its way to the truck

- Panasonic Oxyride batteries: Panasonic targeted the young adult market in the launch of its Oxyride batteries. Apart from regular media buy (TV, print), they maintained significant on-the-ground presence. For example, they would put up tents on campuses and allow student to play Oxyride games, try Oxyride merchandise; in other words, they offered real-life interaction with the brand.

- Cars in malls: Many car dealers place shiny new models on mall floors, sometimes for a specific promotion (enter information to win this car), or sometimes just for the sheer *awareness* factor.

Why are these efforts successful in generating WOM? Because they actually emulate what Small Businesses can and do on a regular basis. Let's examine the elements of the above campaigns using the principles we developed in this Small-Business-focused book.

Create the cool factor (Story WOM): Having the opportunity to try something that can usually only be viewed on a webpage or in a TV ad is *cool*. In some cases, the design of the truck or tent set, and the fact that they come to the consumer can be *cooler* than the actual product. After all, how cool can batteries be?

One-on-one relationship: Product sampling allows companies that don't have actual shops, like a battery maker or a direct seller of computers, to have a tangible (though brief), fun interaction with consumers. They present a great way to move people from Neutrals to Promoters.

Freebies (Facilitate WOM): Pictures, contests, shirts, stickers, pens and other stuff people can take with them and expose others to.

Inbound Information Sharing

Corporations use various tools to share information about a company and its products. These efforts can take many forms, from websites, to case studies, to free consultations.

The three main goals of Inbound information sharing are:

① To address questions and concerns of information seekers who are in the consideration phase.

Example 1: An online flower shop makes a 1-800 number available to people who have questions about web offers.

Example 2: A graphic designer offers to visit a potential client and discuss various approaches to a project.

② To promote content that teaches people about the company or a related topic in an easy, interesting and engaging way.

Example 1: A state tourism board uses a banner ad to promote free downloads of podcast guided tours to various tourist attractions.

Example 2: *An online marketing agency offers on their website a white paper on email best practices.*

③ To start a Two-Way Conversation with its target groups.

Example 1: *A physical therapy clinic staff asks the "how did you hear about us" question, as a conversation starter to learn more about their marketing effectiveness.*

Example 2: *An online adolescent jewelry boutique wants to hear more from their clientele. They create a Blog on their website where young people can comment. They also operate message boards that allow their clients to chat about their favorite gems. A company rep occasionally joins the conversation, making comments and answering questions.*

Inbound Information Sharing just makes sense. When people are already looking for information about a company or a certain topic, providing it to them in a relevant and engaging manner creates an opportunity to build a relationship with the company and alleviate any concerns. Apart from cost, there is no reason not to do it. Companies have created various tools to share more information about themselves. Some use some basic tools, like adding an FAQ section or providing access to sales or customer service representatives. Other have been more sophisticated, providing case studies, live webinars and click-to-chat functionality. All these activities still fall within the corporate 'comfort zone'. Corporations maintain absolute control of the information. Furthermore, what's being described is not complicated: What we do, how we do it, and so on.

That world is quickly changing. It sounds cliché to remind companies that the customer is in the driving seat. Technologies that allow us to instantly post our thoughts about products where many people can read them are growing at a breathtaking pace. Whether it's forwarding an email to "everybody that I know", or posting a product review at Eopinions.com, the rate of growth and adoption of technology keeps surprising industry observers like me.

When power shifts to consumers, it essentially means that a company is not necessarily the first and most-trusted source of information about its own products. There are many other options. Tiny media outlets, like a comment in a message board or a forwarded email, can sink surprisingly big ships. On the flip side, small companies can develop a devout group of followers and make a big splash quickly. Like it or not, people are talking about companies, and the volume is steadily increasingly.

Companies are staring down a major fork in the road: Should they join in the conversation? Its one thing to create a cool website with flashy graphics, but how can they address specific concerns that arise beyond the reach of their own publicity vehicles? The boardrooms of corporations around the world are buzzing with discussions about this challenge. Every CEO must determine whether they are ready for a message board where people can discuss their products and ask questions. Should it be free for all or should they edit the content? Is editing even possible? What about the potential for backlash? The same goes for Blogs. At this point, companies usually create Blogs to achieve specific pre-determined public relations goals; but a Blog is just a letter that is sent in frequent intervals between a company and its customers. Will more regular conversations with customers happen using this tool, even if there are no specific problems to solve?

The answer to all of these questions is a decisive **yes**. Companies will be dragged kicking and screaming into the blogsphere, if only as they react to other information sources that are out there. The fight against potentially negative WOM will be round one. Soon thereafter, companies will begin experimenting with how to use those tools to their advantage. It seems that moving from defense to offence in the WOM front requires a new set of tools and a new approach to marketing; but does it? A proactive approach involves creating great products, admitting that all is not perfect, and being ready to make improvements pronto. That sounds like marketing 101. Doing things right is a defensible position against negative WOM. What's more, it is the basis for Natural WOM and the platform for Amplified WOM.

Inbound Information Sharing:
What most corporations are willing to disclose so far
------ In descending order -------

What is being shared	Rationale
Product description	Satisfying technical or legal requirements: A must have.
FAQ	Trying to clarify issues.
1-800 Sales rep *or* Click-to-chat	The most interactive forum on the face of it, however can be limited by unqualified reps or scripts that lack detail.
Direct Customer feedback (by filling a form or sending an email)	Both a pressure valve, market-research opportunity and actual compliant-resolution mechanism.
Webinar, case studies, testimonials, white papers	More color commentary with a 'real' feel. Still, top-down promotional material.
Blog	Gives the company a human voice (appearance of being unscripted). May or may not allow people to freely post comments.
Consumer generated media	Giving customer the ability to create commercials or taglines for a campaign. A fun and easy way for a company to share its power.
Message boards, chat rooms	Freely allow, and even encourage, consumers to share information about an experience with the company.
Link to external information sources that have good *and* bad reviews	Communicates that "we have nothing to hide!" Not many companies doing this yet. This will change...

Inbound Product Sampling

Product sampling has two main goals for corporations:

1. Draws attention to a new product.
2. Helps bridge the gap between consideration and an actual purchase.

Test drives, trial periods, freeware are all designed to achieve these goals. Similarly, watching vivid images on several televisions in an electronics shop or tasting a new product in a supermarket are examples of product sampling. Corporations usually focus on the sampler with the idea that the more a potential customer "plays" with the product and is pleased with the results, the more likely a person is to actually buy the product. True. The WOM effect of product sampling is often considered a great potential outcome, but usually strategies to amplify WOM are *not* included.

From a holistic WOM perspective, product sampling has four main goals:

① Trying to get more people to sample:

> ‣ Marketing 101: Create awareness and motivate shoppers.

② To encourage samplers to tell others about their experience:

> ‣ WOM about the sampling experience itself, as well as the product.

③ To encourage those who heard about the sampling opportunity to tell others:

> ‣ While I am not interested in test riding a mountain bike on a nature trail, I may know somebody who is interested in this 'sampling opportunity'.

④ To facilitate how current customers can "share" their product with others:

> ‣ If I ask somebody about their cool watch and they show it to me, I am essentially doing a form of product sampling.

These incremental WOM goals can significantly influence the way companies think about product sampling. Imagine the difference in marketing approach between these three product sampling strategic goals:

① Try to get as many people as possible to sample a product knowing that only 20 percent are actually going to consider the product. Setting a goal that each sampler will, on average, drive 1.5 other, new samplers (by telling them about the opportunity to sample).

Versus ➤

② Trying to create buzz around a product-sampling opportunity by making samplers jump through various hoops before they get to sample. The goal is to make people talk about it, but limit the actually sampling to those who are serious.

Versus ➤

③ Try to focus only on warm leads. Maximize conversion of samplers into new customers.

Making It Happen

This section contains a particularly long list of tactics that you may, at some point, want to consider. Some of them have received a lot of press. How will you know what you need to do? I won't dive deeply into how to make it happen (e.g. pros and cons), but there are many resources to help you (an Internet search is usually the best place to start). Keep your focus on strategy (do I need this?) rather than tactics (how will I do it?), at least initially.

Inbound Information Sharing

There are three main goals for Inbound Information Sharing:

1. Address the questions and concerns of information seekers who are in the consideration phase.
2. Make it easy, interesting and engaging to learn more about the company or a topic related to the company.
3. Start a Two-Way Conversation with target groups.

Overall: Blogs, RSS (Real Simple Syndication) are tools, but what do you want to use them for? While they can be useful in addressing various goals, there is nothing unique or magical about them. Here are some new ways to look at info sharing using some tools that you may or may not have considered.

Phone number

In previous chapters, we have talked about what to say to prospective customers on the phone; but sometimes you are not there. What kind of greeting should you record on your answering machine and what does it say about you? I suggest leaving a message that contains information and is relevant, fun and even conversation worthy. Try this on for size: "You have reached Dog Training Unlimited. We invite you to shake paws with us at our new facility. Beginner classes start every week! In the meantime, you can leave us a message after the beep."

FAQ

A Frequently Asked Questions section is a great way to address common concerns and show that you listen and care. Many FAQ sections I have seen were based more on a guessing exercise than on actual questions or concerns harvested from customers or shoppers. A good FAQ should be the result of the great Two-way conversations you are having (Chapter 9).

A good FAQ has the following characteristics:

① The questions are written in a language that is appropriate to the target population; not too formal, not too colloquial. Try to write copy that sounds like the company didn't actually write it.

② FAQs should not just shed a positive light. If there are real concerns about your products, it is better that *you* address them than leave it to others. Be reasonable, fair and admit clear shortcomings, if they exist.

③ Have fun writing FAQs so people will have fun reading them. Include some quirky questions or answers. Showcase your confidence by not taking things too seriously (if this is appropriate for your business).

④ Showcase your story. FAQs are a great opportunity to give people information about you that might be conversation worthy. This might be your story (Chapter 7), or what is it about your company that deserves WOM (Chapter 8).

About Us

I recommend a similar approach to abovementioned FAQs. Many 'About Us' sections simply list facts about the company and its services. It's functional, but mundane. A well-created 'About Us' section can turn into a reason to spend more time on a website or brochure, and even lead to WOM. For example, allowing people to learn something about you or your employees. Letting people see who is actually working for your company – and what they are all about – makes a personal connection; and a personal connection is one of the most important building blocks of WOM. Big brands with multiple products and service associates will have a hard time doing that.

Your 'About Us' section is also the place to get really creative in telling your story (Chapter 7). When people decide to read about you, it is the optimal moment to let them know what is conversation-worthy about you and your business. Their motivation to read this section can be turned into progressive waves of WOM. For example, is any part of the section (text, video, and graphics) interesting enough for people to want to forward it? If so, make that easy to do. Moreover, suggest they do so. "Do you know anyone who would also think what we do is cool? Feel free to email this link to them!" Ask and (at least there is some chance) you shall receive.

Customer Concern/Complaint Channel

As a business owner, you really need to show that you crave to know what's working and what's not. Many businesses still provide customer feedback cards that, on rare occasion, are actually filled out and returned. A fresh approach is needed to motivate people to tell you when things go amiss, or even when they are working well. In my opinion, motivation to give you feedback is ignited only if people believe that somebody actually cares about what they have to say. Simply put, they want to know that someone will read their comments and do something about it. To achieve that, you will need to mention in a meaningful way (website, in conversation, and so on) what changes you have made based on feedback. Only then can you legitimately ask for more feedback.

Capturing customer comments is an essential component in igniting WOM. First, if people have negative WOM, it is better that they talk to you about it before sharing it with others. Even if they do talk to others, at least you have an opportunity to respond. Second, once they have something positive to mention and actually follow up with you, they are more likely to make a habit of it; praising your business may become part of their conversations. Third, when you make things right based on a compliant, it is an opportunity to create a 'Wow Moment' in customer service. Lastly, listening to customers means that you acquire the information you need to create a better business. A business that is nimble and responsive is conversation worthy.

Website

When creating a website, you will need to decide on your overarching business goals as well your WOM goals.

Potential Website Goals:

① **An online business card**

② **Increase your credibility with people who are already considering you (Pre-sale info)**

③ **Offer unique content to increase the number of visitors and their level of engagement once they visit.**

④ **The website is the business.**

An online business card:

A professional-looking website that provides basic information about you (who you are, what you do, how you can be contacted) is all that most businesses need. Creating an appealing, succinct website that achieves these fundamental goals is harder than it seems. For example, can you fit it all on one page, and what should be the mix of graphics and text? Once you set up base camp, there is always more that you can add to achieve higher goals, including WOM.

Increase your credibility with people who are already considering you (Pre-sale info)

Your credibility is a key ingredient needed to move prospective customers from considering you to actually buying from you. You can achieve higher credibility in two ways:

A. *What you say about your business*

▸ **Customers:**
Mention how many customers you have or how many projects have you have done. The more specific you can be, the more credible you will come across. Also, if you work with any well known companies and individuals, mention that as well.

▸ **Crown jewels projects:**
Are there projects that you are especially proud of?

▸ **Case studies:**
Case studies achieve several goals. To start with, they give specific examples about your achievements. It's one thing to talk about results, and quite another to show them. Case studies are a great place to insert some quotes and endorsements from your clients. They are also a place where you can weave in your company or personal story. As importantly, case studies ensure that people extend their visit to your site. It's fair to say that the more people have positive interactions with you, the more likely they are to begin/continue a relationship with you.

▸ **How you reacted to customer feedback and made changes:**
See the "Customer concern/complaint channel" above.

▸ **Professional content or a Blog created by you.**

Doing the above will position you as an expert. It offers a glimpse of your style, level of professionalism and overall approach.

B. *What others say about you:*

▸ **Testimonials:**
Testimonials are the most powerful way to achieve credibility; but how can you persuade people that these testimonials are real? First, the more data you give about the person praising you, the better. For example, consider adding a full name, a picture, and even contact information for the person you are quoting. Add some negative feedback as well, and include what you have done about it. Being open and transparent about your strengths and weaknesses is a great credibility builder. Even if you keep them plain vanilla, testimonials are a great tool. Just the presence of others on your site lends it some credibility.

▸ **Media coverage of your business:**
Including articles that were published by you, speaking engagements you participated in, conferences where you spoke, or any other published or online mention of your business.

▸ **Showcase any awards or prizes you received.**

▸ **Comments to your Blog:**
A Blog can allow people to post unfiltered comments. If you are comfortable with allowing this conversation to happen on your site, then clearly it is the most reliable source for opinions about you.

**Offer unique content to increase the number of
visitors and their level of engagement once they visit**

Having unique content on your website can achieve several goals:

① Drive search traffic to your site.

② Function as a marketing tool.

③ Encourage site visitors to extend their stay.

④ Support dissemination of your web address by visitors to others.

Some businesses use the content on their site to drive search traffic to it. For example, a water purification device maker might post several articles in order to increase the odds that their website will appear among the top search results when someone Googles a term like "water purification options".

Unique content can also be a marketing tool. For example, a technology firm can include a section about nanotechnology. The unique information provided in this section can be advertised in various forums. For example, other websites can link to it, Bloggers can link to it, or the company can buy a banner ad on a Nanotechnology site advertising the section.

Unique content ensures that visitors will stay longer at your site and start to become familiar with your company. When considering a purchase, a stronger engagement with a brand or a company can definitely make a difference. Unique content can make your website a destination all its own that perhaps can result in WOM. This would be a phenomenal result; marketing space on your own site to information seekers is abundant and free (it's your site).

Let's review several options for content:

Static Web Pages: As the headline suggests, these are web pages that you create once in a major "project" and only add or modify occasionally. You can choose basic web page text and graphics, or take a slightly more sophisticated approach that includes case studies, testimonials or other features mentioned above.

White Papers: White Papers are essentially essays, presentations or reports that are created in a PDF, Word format, or appear as a web page. A White Paper can cover many topics: survey results, research performed, tips and tricks, best practices, deep discussion of a topic, overview of industry latest news, and so on. Clearly, the overwhelming majority of businesses out there don't have unique knowledge that can be shared in this way. If that's you, just skip over this mini section.

White papers can usually be downloadable (and then forwarded to others). More sophisticated websites allow a visitor to email the White Paper to themselves, as well as to other friends or contacts. Both methods constitute the beginning of a viral campaign.

A relevant, timely White Paper can be advertised on its own merit. The idea is that instead of promoting your company and its offering, you are promoting your White Paper. With the explosion in the number of websites and Blogs, everybody is in search of great content. The chances of your website being mentioned or linked to because of some well-created content are much higher than just for your product offering alone.

Blog: A Blog is essentially an online diary. It can be a website by itself, or an area in a website. Many people read Blogs on a regular basis and don't even know it. In many cases, Blogs don't look or feel much different than regular static websites.

Blogs require a lot of work to maintain. Some post once a month, some post several times a day. It also requires content that is interesting and different enough to be picked up by other sites or by web searchers. In fairly rare cases, a Blog can actually develop a group of devoted followers who check in on a regular basis.

Similar to the advice I give about White Papers, I want to remind you that most businesses don't have unique knowledge that can be translated to a Blog. Even if they have some, it can appear in static webpages (or other forms). Very few have something to say every day or even once a week. In industries undergoing significant and rapid change, Bloggers can offer insights about relevant topics; these industries (e.g. Search Marketing or Alternative Fuels) are the exception. Consultants who actually sell knowledge are another group. Also, if the product a company is selling is very complex, a Blog is a great space to continuously address questions and concerns.

There are other possible benefits to Blogs. Some Bloggers actually make money from their Blog (mostly by selling advertising on it). Many Bloggers write entries that involve reviewing other websites or Blogs. When they do, they provide links to those sites. In return, they expect to be linked to them once in a while. This has two effects: First, it immediately increases traffic to their site. Second, incoming links increase the relevancy of their page as determined by the Search Engine, and is therefore likely to appear nearer the top when people search for terms relevant to what the company is writing about.

Podcast: A podcast is a way to share information about you or from you in an audible form. I've heard of several applications that make sense. Places of worship giving access to weekly sermons by podcasts, or museums making available guided tours for people walking around their exhibits. Can a podcast really allow you to do something you can't achieve with a regular website? Do you believe that your target market uses Ipods and can be motivated to download your podcasts? If you are pondering it and 'no' isn't your clear answer, it might be worth testing podcasting for a while. Technically speaking, it is not that complex to add one to your site.

The website is the business

For example, an E-commerce site that sells a product or an eBay business. How to create a website for these purposes is outside the scope of this book, but there are numerous online resources to help you do that.

Potential Website WOM goals

① **Availability**

Once people have heard about you and are looking for you, it is imperative that they can locate you easily. You want to appear in a simple name search online or in the yellow/super pages. This is not as straight forward as it sounds, because you don't exactly know what it is that people will remember about you and use when searching for you. You will have to do some reconnaissance to find that out. You can do that by first asking people what they looked for when they searched for you, and second, using some basic web analytics to determine what search terms lead to your website.

There are certain situations where what people remember about you is hard to convert to actually finding you. For example, you are a consultant and share your first and last name with many other famous and not-so-famous folks. Or people remember what you do or the city you are in, but not your business name specifically. That is the time to consider using a Pay Per Click strategy, where you actually pay Google/Yahoo/MSN to ensure you appears near the top section of its pages.

② **Website is WOM Worthy**
Is there something WOM worthy about the website itself? Why would people forward a link or talk about it? Clearly, a website is the most flexible platform to present any of your WOM-generating ideas. Whether it's your story, building WOM into your business, or anything else cool and exciting, a website can be the forum for it. There are some special features a website has (most were mentioned above) that can make it more WOM ready. For example, unique information in a Blog or a White Paper is just asking to be forwarded. Or it can be as simple as the look and feel. The bottom line is that *website goals and WOM web goals are not the same.* A website can be functional and well designed, but that does not necessarily make it conversation worthy or email-forwardable. If it is worth your time to create a website that is more than an online business card, it is worth the time to explore ideas that would encourage people to forward your site or its content to others.

③ **Facilitate WOM**
Key question: *How can you encourage and make it easy to forward your site and its contents to others?* In essence, encouraging people to forward information about you is similar to every other direct-response marketing effort.

- *Outline a Unique Selling Point:*
  In WOM marketing, you are not necessarily promoting what you sell. To be clear, your product or service might be the first reason why people forward your site, but there may be other things about it (cool content, relevant information) that also motivates them. Also, people who are probably never to going to be your customers need a pretty good reason to forward it to others who *are* potential customers. Sounds like a lot of work? A brief call to action (see below) is probably all you need.

- *A call to action is must.*
  It is imperative in every direct-response marketing effort to ask people directly to take the action you are hoping for. In this case: To forward things to their friends. Consider this piece of copy for a company providing conference call services:
  "Thinking about using a conference call service? Click here to download our Complete Getting Started Guide. Know somebody else who might be interested? Click here to send them a copy now!"

- *Ask in many ways and many places.*
  A call to action, reasons why people should respond, and suggestions about how others would benefit should appear in various places on the page. Homepage, other pages, buttons, boxes, free text, and so on. Also, try asking in various ways using different copy. A portfolio of approaches might hit the mark with a broader cross section of readers.

- *Make it easy to forward.*
  An easy-to-remember website address is a great start. Plus, there

are a variety of other tools you include on your website, like an "Email to a friend button", or White papers in Word or PDF formats that are easy to send. To stay ahead of the curve, you will need to do more than the basics. For example, almost every site has a refer-a-friend button. Can you make yours bigger and bolder? Can you create a text box pointing to it and mention why people should forward? Think outside of the box to make referrals happen for you.

Inbound Product Sampling

Most SB owners would agree that persuading people who are interested in your company to take the next step and *experience* your company is an important step in converting them into customers. *Experiencing* your company can take many forms. A wedding planner can bring a (future) bride and groom to a wedding to view her style. A hairdresser might offer the first haircut at 70 percent off. Every business can come up with ways to let people sample its offering. But that's not all. In the same way people WOM about products, they also WOM about samples and the sampling experience. In fact, sampling a product can be a lot more conversation worthy than the thing itself. First, there is something exciting about getting something for "free" or close to free. Second, there is an aura of excitement around something "new". *New* and *free* are some of the most common words used in advertising. Finally, sampling is an involved form of consideration and evaluation. When people have various options to choose from, or they dive deeper into one option, they feel the need to get advice and share their quandaries with others. Viola! WOM is created.

Earlier, we identified the four key goals of a holistic WOM approach to Inbound Product Sampling:

① Trying to get more people to sample:
  ‣ Marketing 101: Creating awareness and motivate shoppers.
② To encourage samplers to tell others about their experience:
  ‣ WOM about the sampling experience itself, as well as the product.
③ To encourage those who heard about the sampling opportunity to tell others:
  ‣ For example, I am not interested in test riding a mountain bike on a nature trail, but I may know somebody who is.
④ To facilitate how current customers can "share" their product with others:
  ‣ For example, if I ask somebody about their cool watch and they show it to me, I am essentially doing a form of product sampling.

How do these goals translate into the real world of business? Initially, it is important to notice that smaller businesses are much more likely to get people to sample their products than bigger businesses. Even a simple conversation with the business owner is a form of product sampling. A lot can be learned from a customer perspective in such an interaction. The benefit to the owner is that once somebody has already completed this form of sampling, they are somewhat "hooked". It is much harder to say 'no' to a person than to a website or a faceless corporate entity. Also, many businesses have on-the-ground local operations that can more easily offer a sampling experience.

Let's use the WOM framework to guide the approach to Inbound Product Sampling WOM marketing:

Initially, every business needs to think about how they can create a "bite size chunk" that others can sample. The first goal is to create a no-risk, hassle-free, or low-cost opportunity for a test drive. The second goal is to make either the concept of the sampling, or the sampling itself conversation worthy. This exercise is very similar to the principles we discussed in the chapter concerning Story WOM. Consider this idea: For its grand opening, a small coffee shop decides to collaborate with a local high school. Coffee will be served by the high school's mascot, football players and cheerleaders (all proceedings go the team). Or a more wacky idea: A handbag shop "rents" totes on a weekly basis. After a few weeks, women can decide which one suits them the most and purchase. In both cases, I would argue that the sampling concept is more conversation worthy than the actual product.

Product sampling is costly, so make sure that you understand the segments you want to focus on. Try to think about making sampling available to those who are most likely to become customers. For example, when somebody calls to get more information, you are probably already assessing whether they are worth more of your time and effort. Similarly, if you happen to advertise product sampling, chose media that is most likely to reach your target market. By the way, product sampling can be selective, or even offered as a prize. Test driving a sports car sounds more like a prize than a product sampling opportunity. Think about whether you can use being selective about who can sample to your advantage. Exclusivity (manifested in limited time offers, competitions, and so on) is a classic driver of WOM.

Facilitating sampling WOM – encouraging people to talk about the sampling they have done – is the next step. The most obvious approach is to give samplers invitations that they can forward to others (Email, paper, freebies). Get creative. For example, what will samplers take away with them after sampling? A landscaper can tour recent projects with a prospective client and make a portfolio of photos. If it is on disk or in an email, it can be forwarded. Also, consider some kind of refer-a-friend program for the sampling piece itself (we cover RAF at length in chapter 16). The most simple one is something along the lines of, "bring a friend to sample and receive a gift/further discount." Another basic tactic is to mention that you can only sample if someone referred you. Try to think outside the box for other rewards that might entice people to mention the sampling experience to others. Finally, and most importantly: Don't forget to ask people to WOM! Something as simple as a one-on-one request to talk to others might provide a fairly big bang for your time and effort around sampling. Ask for WOM and there is at least a chance (greater than zero) it will happen.

Make sure that you evaluate your efforts. Ask the, "How did you hear about our sampling?" question in the same way you ask, "How did you hear about us?"

Noting how you got most of your samplers can give you direction on where to focus more of your time and where to spend less.

Last but far from least, think about how your customers can become a walking product sampling opportunity. There are several businesses who take full advantage of this prospect. Contractors put signs on lawns when they perform work. Any product that is worn or displayed has a chance to be noticed or experienced, and thus talked about. Is there a creative way that you can work with your customers so that their use of your product will highlight your company and make your presence visible to others?

Outbound: *Definition* (reminder): Actively reaching out to others.

Outbound Information Sharing and Product Sampling

Even businesses that don't spend any money on advertising or marketing should make an effort to present themselves or their products to people in some forum. Many small business owners try to write articles about their trade to local newspapers or to be interviewed by them. Some try to find opportunities for speaking engagements. Others try to present their products using stands at community events. At a more basic level, whenever a serious client appears on the horizon, owners are ready to reach out and make an extra phone call or visit to seal the deal. Owners also network (see chapter 10), which is a process that includes letting people know about what they do.

The goal of all the activities above is to enable the owner to let as many people know about the business as possible. Encouraging those who hear about you to tell others takes marketing to the *next level*. The small business advantage is that most interactions happen on a personal level, usually face to face. Common sense suggests that a personal interaction is more likely to generate WOM than an interaction with a faceless brand.

Apart from making their presentation or story conversation worthy, the focus on outbound work should be on how to facilitate WOM. There are a couple of best practices that businesses can follow to get the most from their efforts:

- **Sound bytes:**
  Make sure that, by design, there are some highlights in your presentation that you believe (or have received feedback) are conversation worthy. They need to be short and memorable (explained in fewer than 30 seconds).
- **Suggest a follow up for direct listeners:**
  - Outline all the ways that you can be reached. The information should be presented in a way that even a semi-senile person can remember, even if they don't write anything down.
  - Ask people if they want to join an email list to receive updates.
  - Mention your website.
  - Hand out something (e.g. flyer or card) that contains the above info.

- **Ask them to talk to others:**
  - ▸ Make sure that you clearly ask for their help in taking your business to the next level by telling others about it.
  - ▸ Make the case for why telling others is a win-win for everybody (customers and the business). Tell them about your goals, your dreams and your aspirations for the company. Tell them how the company benefits employees and the community as a whole.
  - ▸ Similar to the above points, make sure that you make it easy for them to follow up with others and tell them how to reach you

Chapter Summary – *What you need to know*

☑ Businesses routinely share information about their business (websites, brochures, speaking engagements, advertising, answering calls or emails etc) and let people sample their products (trial periods, free first meeting with prospective client etc).

☑ The challenge in these activities is not only how to promote the business efficiently but also how to encourage people who consume information or sample the company's products to talk about what they learned to others.

☑ There are various tactics to transform tools like answering machine messages and website features to WOM generators. Having WOM as a goal for these tools significantly changes the perspective to their design.

☑ Persuading people to sample your product is a great step towards making them into a customer. The goal should also be that those 'experimenters' would be such a conversation-worthy experience that they will just have to share the news with others.

☑ Some business owners actively reach out to others by writing articles or participating in speaking engagements. To take their marketing efforts using these tools to the next level, owners should try to encourage readers or listeners to relay their message forward. This can be done by creating unique, sound byte size highlights in their story, suggesting direct follow ups, and making the case about why readers/listeners should tell others about the information.

Exercises

☑ Create a list of all the marketing efforts that you currently do.

- *Brainstorm about what you can change or emphasize in these efforts to enable them to be WOM generators.*
- *Think about how you would make it easy for others to tell others about you (facilitate WOM), and how would it be easy for listeners to find you.*

12 CREATING A REFERENCE/ RECOMMENDATION PROGRAM

The Big Idea

Many resumes finish with the phrase, "references available upon request." Does your business have references or people who are willing to talk about it to potential buyers? Such people are a great asset for every business. A Reference/ Recommendation Program is different from a refer-a-friend program in that a Recommendation Program includes some *formal* agreement that the Referee either provide WOM (e.g. indicate they are willing to accept calls from prospective customers) or is willing to be highlighted in a case study or customer testimonial.

There are multiple WOM opportunities in this sort of initiative. First, not many businesses have this kind of program; the fact that yours does by itself might be worth a conversation. Second, what references say and who they are can also generate buzz. Most importantly, third parties are a more credible, less biased source of information about you, and people will trust that. Everybody understands that references are going to be at least somewhat biased. However, if they come across as reputable sources, the fact that a business *has* these kinds of clients or peers is a reassuring sign.

Making references available for a direct conversation is only one way to gain value from this approach. Success stories, case studies and customer testimonials can be shared in various forms of communication to gain maximum credibility and generate WOM. When it comes to facilitating WOM, new technologies described in the "Information Sharing" chapter allows for easy sharing of these customer-based stories with others (brochures, emails, case studies on the website that can be forwarded/downloaded, and so on). At the same time, mentioning the availability of references in a first sales call might be all the technology you need.

What Big Corporations Do

The beacon for Referral Programs are Business-to-Business (B2B) companies (we discuss those at length in Chapter 6 about networking).

References are essential for B2Bs that sell large-ticket items to a small set of potential customers (other companies). B2B marketers know very well that before making a purchase, companies will tap into various networks to get the "scoop" on the company's products and services. A Reference/Recommendation Program is a way to address concerns without any form of 'direct marketing'. Also, it is an opportunity to shorten the purchasing cycle. In WOM terms, a Reference program is a way to ensure that more people are talking more favorably about you to the a target market B2Bs care about – new customers.

Making It Happen

It could be that you are already doing a great job selling your services and you are also a great WOM generator. Yet, when *others* talk about you using the same or similar messages, they are likely to be more effective. Essentially, a Reference/Recommendation group is a way to ensure WOM, or in other words, a structured WOM program.

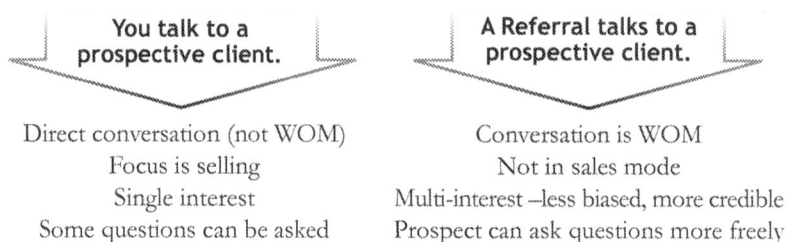

You talk to a prospective client.	A Referral talks to a prospective client.
Direct conversation (not WOM)	Conversation is WOM
Focus is selling	Not in sales mode
Single interest	Multi-interest –less biased, more credible
Some questions can be asked	Prospect can ask questions more freely

Steps to building a Reference/Recommendation program:

Build your pool of references:

- Approach current Promoters or Evangelists or former clients.
- Make sure that they have no outstanding issues with regard to your business. Similarly, make sure that you understand and make up for any negative experiences they have had in the past.
  - ▶ You want to avoid the, "Yes, they are great apart from that time when…"
- Ask permission to use them as a reference for new buyers.
- Ask permission to highlight them in a customer testimonial, white paper, or case study (if you are planning to publish those).
- Most importantly, make sure that you explain to your reference group how *they* will benefit form being part of the program: Publicity, prestige, new business contacts, a future discount or simply the benefit of helping you out.
- Communicate that benefit to the individuals and companies you approach.

Coach your Reference:

- Make sure that you don't come across as trying to influence your references' opinions or message too strongly.
- Instead, offer them advice on how to make their conversations with others more effective.
- For example, supply them information about:
  - ▶ Key concerns people usually have (and how your company addresses them).
  - ▶ Any developments in the business (new products, problems that used to exist and are now solved).
- Re-iterate the benefits of being part of the program as you coach.

Using your Reference/Recommendation group:

- Companies are very careful about when to give actual contact information (e.g. providing the phone number of a reference), and when to just present success stories. The criterion is self evident: Potential big accounts get royal treatment and more access. Smaller clients get the brochure, or can read recommendations online.
- Think clearly about the right time to use references in the buying process: Early versus later.

  Early:

  Pros: Gives you instant credibility; might be especially important if the company is very small and unknown, or people have major concerns that need to be addressed before using the company's services.

  Cons: The ratio of sales to people talking to references might be small. If somebody is going to contact one of your references, you want the conversation to count. For example, a person might be early in their decision-making process, and thus not have all their questions lined up. Similarly, you want to make sure you avoid overusing your contacts. If the potential buyer is not ready to have a serious conversation with the reference and leaves them feeling that it had no impact, it is a lose-lose. If you have a situation where you get a lot of inquiry calls (and don't want to fatigue your references), make sure that you can "commoditize" recommendations about you. You can do that by providing testimonials and case studies and forward this information (using brochures, email, or a website).

  Later:

  Pros: Avoids overusing references by saving them for more serious and knowledgeable buyers. This can make a conversation with a reference much more satisfying for both parties.

  Cons: If your challenge is that you get quite a few inquires, but have trouble converting them into serious shoppers, you might be using references too late in the process. A quick fix: Mention that references are available, but only after a buyer goes through several steps (for example, a conversation with a sales rep, a site visit, or a review of services). Capture the cache references offer, but buy yourself some time and use them with only a selected few serious customers.

Show your appreciation to those who refer/recommend:

- Compensation can be a personal 'thank you card', or even something more substantial, like a discount for future purchases or a gift card.
- Keep them happy and not over worked.
- Continuously assess the situation so as to give them a break before they get frustrated.

Final considerations:

- Keep it ethical:
  - ▶ Don't use family or friends as fake referrals.
- Keep it real:
  - ▶ People tune out over-the-top endorsements.
  - ▶ Consider posting some bad comments on your website/brochure alongside the actions you took to resolve them.
  - ▶ Overall, make sure that you come across as a reasonably credible entity.

Chapter Summary – *What you need to know*

☑ A Reference/Recommendation program is a formal agreement with clients who agree to either:

- *Receive calls from people interested in doing business with you (to learn about you), or*
- *Be the focus of a case study, white paper or testimonial quote.*

☑ Program can lead to increased levels of WOM because:

- *Program might be something unique and worth a conversation by itself.*
- *Conversation with a program participant is a way to guarantee WOM (the conversation itself is WOM).*
- *Usually, referrers are considered to be somewhat less biased than you about your own business.*

☑ A successful program includes several key elements including:

- *Deciding when in the purchasing cycle (for example, initial call versus just before the deal is closed) to use you references to avoid overuse.*
- *Coaching them about your business to make them feel "in the loop", maintaining the relationship and making sure that they have the latest data.*
- *Showing your appreciation and motivating references.*
- *Being ethical: Don't use non customers (like family and friends).*

Exercises

- ☑ Try to think about whether you believe that you would gain some value from a Reference/Recommendation programs.

- ☑ If yes, start small but get active. Who can be the first two or three people you can call to put on your list?

- ☑ Begin using these references for a few weeks and try to asses the impact of their conversations with prospective clients on results.
  - *Simply ask: "Did you call one of my references? How did the conversation go?"*
  - *Similarly, loop back with your references and ask about their conversations so far.*

The Big Idea

Viral marketing happens when content (video, picture, text) is created by an individual or company and is "spread" to others. "Going Viral" means creating a message designed to be forwarded again and again. Anyone who has ever used email has received viral messages. Most of us have also forwarded emails, which makes us part of Viral marketing.

A Viral campaign begins with seeding. If Nike creates a video it wants people to forward, it can choose from a variety of places where we can see it first. It can post the video on sites like YouTube or BoreMe. It can email it to people. It can also send it to Bloggers, website editors, and sports-themed websites. Or, it can advertise a mini Nike website that hosts the video.

Because WOM marketing is such a new concept, there are people out there who believe that Viral marketing is all there is to WOM marketing. Those people, as a rule, often dismiss the WOM concept as not being relevant to them. If you are reading this, you know that is not the case. I understand why people dismiss Viral marketing. It's true that the Viral content that has received the most attention has been funny, bizarre or controversial (see the ten most popular Viral Videos later in the chapter). It's also true that the target market for early Viral videos was a younger audience with limited purchasing power.

None of this changes the fact that content you create will be passed around if it's relevant, unique and cool. Think back to the emails you have received in the past. Have you forwarded emails or web links to friends or family that were not funny or bizarre? I'm confident that the answer is yes. Viral marketing may be a tactic that you use only once in a while, or not at all; but it is something businesses need to consider. Creativity and 'out of the box' thinking will help you reach unexpected levels of success.

What Big Corporations Do

The approach most big corporations took to developing Viral campaigns was similar to how they approached regular brand advertising: Funny (e.g. Burger King's subservient chicken), celebrities (Nike used Brazilian soccer star Rhonaldinio kicking a ball to the crossbar four times), or the bizarre (Best Buy's video of a cheerleader being thrown into a basketball hoop). For a marketer, achieving brand awareness (aided and unaided) is an important result. Videos achieve this goal if they go viral. However, greater awareness of a brand does not directly influence whether people will consider buying. Nevertheless, the argument here is basic: People can't consider you if they don't know you exist. And in any case, if a Viral video is a way to reach more eyeballs in a cheaper, more targeted way than TV ads (which are mostly about brand awareness), then it is a viable option to explore.

Corporations tried to take this one step further and allow for consumers to generate ads. For example, Chevrolet encouraged customers to create ads for their Tahoe truck and share them with friends. Some were positive ads, but others were negative, even vulgar. The program was fairly quickly cancelled, but some unsavory videos still exist in various video hosting sites. GM knew and accepted that unleashing control might result in some bad videos. What they did not expect was the volume of publicity these negative videos would receive. The lesson: When the customer is in control, it's hard to predict the results. In this case, a brand representing a big SUV will attract some hostility, representing a risk. Brands that are more universally liked will have an easier time putting customers in the driver's seat.

Though investment in Viral marketing by corporations is sky rocketing because of the perceived low-cost-high-reach of this method, many businesses are still timid about joining the party. There are several good reasons for that. First, conservative companies just don't consider funny, bizarre videos to be part of their brand image; other companies are afraid of the wild-wild-west aspect of the online world. When a company creates a video, it can be easily manipulated by those hostile to the brand and morph into something very different (and not surprisingly, more popular).

I believe that every company can use Viral Marketing. The challenge is that they need to create content that people will be motivated to spread for reasons others than it being strange or funny. The market for humorous messages is quickly becoming saturated.

Making It Happen

Forget about massive success; start small first. Even if one of your business emails gets forwarded several times and a few more people learn about you (or enhance their knowledge of you), you have achieved a low-cost-high impact marketing result. This may have already happened for you with past e-mails. So how do you make sure that more people forward more of your messages to more people?

Many businesses use email to communicate with customers. Broadly speaking, there are two kinds of email communications: Broadcast email and person-to-person email.

Broadcast email is either an email you send to a group of people, or an automated email. In both cases, it is not highly customized. A group email can be an e-newsletter you send every month, or an announcement you make about a new product or a change in the business. Some businesses send regular customer service or statement emails. Automated email comes in many forms. For many e-commerce businesses (such as eBay businesses), an automated email is generated immediately after a sale. However, most email is created ad-hoc. A Broadcast email can be customized to the needs or preferences of various groups; however, it is still addressed to a group of people, which affects its look and feel.

Person-to-person email is perhaps more likely to be read, but is also more time consuming than Broadcast email. Most people are more likely to open an email from someone they know than from a company. The advantage Small Businesses have over corporations is that they often have closer relationships that enable them to send genuine person-to-person emails. How can you create emails that sound personal and distribute them widely without much effort? Create message or content and leave some room at the top or bottom to add a personal message.

Before we dive more deeply into tactics, let me spend a minute on ethical emailing. Broadcast emails should only be sent to customers or people who opt to receive emails from you. You should always verify that people have "opted in" and make available the opportunity to opt out. Spam is not just wrong; it can get you into all kinds of trouble (damage people's impression of you, create legal problems, and so on).

Make sure that your email is opened

Every email you send represents an opportunity for WOM to be created. The first order of business is to make sure that the basic premise of the email is important enough for people to open it. There are various levers that you should consider that will increase the likelihood others will open your email (tag lines, format, graphics, to name a few). Just Google "email marketing best practices" and see what's applicable to you. Even so, person-to-person email requires much less technical work.

Embedding the Viral Message

Once somebody opens your email, how will you encourage them to forward it to others? Start by deciding whether you want a Viral message to be the main focus of an email, or if you want to include viral elements in emails that have a broader purpose. I suggest testing both. In fact, the low cost of email allows to you test various content and creative executions to see what works.

Find a reason to forward

Ignite your imagination! Here are a few ideas to get you started:
What is Viral:

- Special offers you send to Customers (and they forward to Non-Customer friends and colleagues).
- A coupon or discount.
- A product or service launch (e.g. "We are coming to your area.").
- An event that you create or sponsor (community or professional).
- An invitation to sample ("You already enjoy our widgets, but do you know anybody who would like to sample our latest development, widgets 2.0, at our special testing center?").
- An opinion you have about something (either very angry, or very pleased – emphasis on 'very').
- A cause you believe in or that you create; include a call to action that requires forwarding.

Think segments

Viral marketing is clearly easier to start with existing customers. They have already opted in and know you. However, don't overlook Non Customers, especially your personal network. Every social or professional group that you are a member of is fair game. Clearly, the email needs to have some relevance to the targeted group. This is not a straight-forward task. Start with some easy-to-implement ideas. For example, think about tag lines like this: "Special offer to soccer club moms," or "Do you know somebody looking for a new widget?" People in your current network or social circles can help ignite the fire of Viral marketing.

Give special attention to Influencers

In the WOM framework, we developed in the beginning of the book, we mentioned that there are four characteristics that might explain why some people are more influential than others: Motivation, credibility, size of social circle and technical ability.

Do you know anybody you would rate highly on one or more of the attributes above? If you do, then these people deserve special attention. First, they warrant a personal email as opposed to being tagged onto a distribution list. Then, capture their attention. You must be clear about what's special about your message and why they should care. Also, make sure that you chose your battles appropriately: Use Influencers infrequently.

Aim high if it makes sense

So far we have focused on starting an email campaign that might result in some forwarding, but is not designed to achieve massive reach. Companies that focus on online sales or are especially creative might dream of being noticed by thousands, or even millions of people. Considering that many Viral videos are homemade (or at least look that way) means everybody can do it. Ask any teenager for help.

Here is an example: A specialty web site that sells authentic foods from the Netherlands might create a funny Dutch-themed video and send it around the Dutch community abroad. Brand awareness is important for them and can be achieved with a video that only their target market will understand and identify with.

Make it easy to forward:

- Ask people to pass the message on near the beginning of the email. Make sure people hear a clear call to action.

- Give them a good reason to forward the message (it would make them look clever, it provides useful information, or it's amusing).

- Don't include heavy graphics, fancy HTML or attachments that can potentially be blocked by some recipients (test your email with a few friends before sending it broadly).

- Use links instead of attachments.

- Use links to your website for people to learn more about you.

- Repeat your call to action at end of the message (add a P.S. section after the signature; this is a direct mail 'best practice').

Top ten Viral videos from *Time Magazine*:

1. Star War Kid (playing with a light saber)
2. Numa Numa (guy enjoys singing Romanian pop)
3. David Elsewhere (boneless breakdancer)
4. Ronaldinho (soccer stunts)
5. Lazy Sunday (Saturday Night Live's Samberg and Parnell)
6. Jon Versus Tucker (the ultimate TV host showdown)
7. Brokeback to the Future (Brokeback Mountain meets Back to the Future)
8. Basketgirl! (A girl is thrown through a basketball hoop. My insider sources say it didn't actually happen)
9. Ninja Guy (Stunts)
10. Best Christmas lights ever

Chapter Summary – *What you need to know*

☑ Viral marketing is about the creation of content (story, video, special promotion, etc) that is interesting enough that people will forward it to others, usually by email.

☑ Viral marketing is not just about funny or bizarre videos. Essentially, every time you press the "forward" button in your email, you are part of a viral marketing campaign.

☑ Few companies achieve massive scale Viral marketing reach, but even very small companies can create messages with forwarding potential (e.g. a discount program, a new product or service, etc).

☑ There are two kinds of email:
  - *Broadcast email: An e-newsletter, purchase confirmation, customer statement*
  - *Person-to-person email: Highly customized, feels like a personal email.*

☑ Viral marketing may not be your first choice but you should you consider it – aside from costing you time, it's pretty cheap.

Exercises

☑ Create a Viral marketing test:

- *Create two different email messages. Each one with a different spin or graphical execution. Both should be created with the goal of encouraging recipients to forward them to others.*

- *Take your email list for the test and divide it into two groups. Send email one to group one and email two to group two. Make sure that you have clear documentation of who is in each group and what message they received.*

- *To evaluate if the test works and which email works better, probe people who call or email with questions like, "how did you hear about this?" While not scientific, it will at least give you some measure of success.*

- *A slightly more advanced (and accurate) version of this test is to create two emails that have clearly different information in them (different products, different sales coupons, etc). That way, you can determine which email generates more leads just by taking note of what people call or email about.*

14 YOUR BUZZ TEAM

The Big Idea

Explicitly asking a group of individuals to spread WOM about your business (and their agreement to do just that) is a great way to start your marketing campaign. In fact, that's the way most businesses start. Talk to Small Business owners and they will tell you that their first clients were either family or from their personal network, and that word about them spread from there. The ultimate goal of creating a Buzz team is to become a little bit more deliberate and increase the number of people actively buzzing on your behalf, enabling them to be more effective at it and continuing to motivate them to do so.

What's most important is to push your 'asking' skills to a new level. Persuade yourself that you can weather the results: Some people will say 'yes' and never follow up, and others will even say 'no'. Your friends, family and current personal network might be a great start, but you will have to push it a step further. What's working for you? People, I believe, *want* to be helpful, especially when the request comes in a more intimate one-on-one setting. In the fundraising world, there is an old adage: People give to people, not to organizations. That is the reason that many non-for-profit charities organize buzz teams to call on friends and family to donate.

There is a big debate in the WOM community about whether you should focus on the most influential people you know. They fall into the various categories you might have encountered: Influencers, mavens, trend-setters, connectors, bees. Specialty WOM marketing companies spend significant resources trying to identify these people and determine the best ways to persuade them to spread the word about certain products. There is no doubt that encouraging an extroverted, smart, credible person with hundreds of contacts on her email list to actively talk about your products is the stuff of marketing dreams. There are people like that out there, but how many do you know? Plus, even if you do find someone who fits the bill, will they have the time and energy to support your efforts? I believe that motivation to speak to others about products and services you encounter is as important as any other factor. For the most part, we all use email, we all have a social circle we meet with regularly, and (heaven knows) we all like to give advice to others. Bottom line: Everyone should be considered part of your Buzz team. By contrast, there are professional Influencers, like reporters, Bloggers, or civic leaders, who are worth of the effort it takes to approach them. We will cover this topic in the next chapter.

Motivating your buzz team is another key element of the strategy. They need to know that you appreciate their efforts and that they are making a difference. Give them the satisfaction of telling them that they helped you succeed by bringing new people in. Make people feel like insiders. Let them know about your plans, your next moves, a new project, your story. Many people already like to talk about the products or people that they know. Asking them to join your Buzz group just channels that enthusiasm. A motivated Buzz team will continue to look for opportunities to spread WOM about you over the long haul.

What Big Corporations Do

Many companies that embrace WOM try to recruit a group of people to promote their products to others. Proctor & Gamble is famous for signing up groups of stay-at-home moms or teenagers to both evaluate P&G products and talk about them with friends. These groups are comprised of up to 100,000 people! Software companies rely on user groups to spread the word about new products. There are even companies like BuzzAgent, that have standing armies of people willing to promote products to family and friends. They do so for some form of compensation, or the opportunity to sample products first, or simply to have something to talk about.

Many people are uncomfortable with this development. If we can't trust the recommendations of friends and family, what can we trust? The potential commercialization of chatting focuses us on distinguishing the fine line between promoting a product that you believe in and selling products for financial or other benefit. I personally don't think that there is anything inherently wrong with asking people to mention your company to others, but there are several ethical landmines that should be avoided in this exercise. First, people should only promote products they have a genuine appreciation for. Compensation (in whatever form) should not be so high as to entice people to promote everything and anything. Second, information passed to promoters must be accurate. WOM is an unregulated marketing channel (as compared to direct mail or TV ads). As a result, some companies feel its okay to give their promoters talking points that don't meet the usual standards for accuracy and completeness. That's wrong. Third, stunts and fake WOM are unacceptable. I remember hearing a story on the radio about a company that sends actors to stand in line in banks or post offices and talk about a shop that recently opened next door. That's also clearly wrong.

Making It Happen

Creating a Buzz team is one way to guarantee that WOM will be spread about you and your business. That is not to say that everybody you ask to WOM on your behalf will agree to do so, or that they will actually do it; but even if a percentage of them do, usually the return on your investment of time and energy will be worth it.

Asking for WOM

- Start with a person-to-person approach. People are more likely to agree to WOM if you interact with them on a one-on-one basis. Asking for WOM in a face-to-face conversation or over the phone is probably the most effective, but reaching out to a larger group through a personalized email might work as well.

- When talking to your potential candidates, don't begin by telling them about the products you want them to promote. Instead, present your case for why they should support you (your dream of building a business, what people already say about you, or the industry and how you plan to improve things).

- Tell them how their help can really make a difference.

- If the person you are approaching is already a customer, or had some interaction with your work, a great place to start is a Two-Way Conversation (Chapter 9). In essence, it means asking them for their opinion about your business, then, when they are in the right 'mode', explicitly asking for their WOM support.

- Be very clear about what you are asking them to do (see the Expectations section below).

Creating a Board of Directors

- Every business, however small, should have a group of people who meet regularly to offer advice. Almost every religious or educational institution has one, and you can too.

- Apart from advice, the benefit of a board is that the people on it are motivated to promote your business. Who wouldn't feel proud to say that they are advising businesses or are a member of 'the Board'? Channeling this motivation into WOM might even be the main reason to create this entity.

- Bottom line: Asking people to be on your board is a great way to ask for WOM. Even if a person says 'No' to a board seat (e.g. because they are worried about the time commitment), just asking them should help facilitate future WOM-related conversations.

Who to ask

- Family, friends, customers and your personal network come first.
- Creating a Buzz team should really be looked at as a Networking exercise. Put differently, trying to find people to add to your Buzz team can be a

goal in networking.

- Don't overlook any of your business partners (for example, your suppliers).

Your expectations from your Buzz team

- Be clear about how you expect people to WOM about you, especially if you want them to be proactive.
- Email: Are you going to write the email for them, or will they? Who do you want them to forward the email to?
- Conversations: Are there any specific people or groups you want them to talk to? Or, do you just expect them to mention you when a relevant topic comes up in a conversation?
- Can they take part in your more structured, organized WOM?
  - ▸ Can they give out Freebies?
  - ▸ Tell others about sampling opportunities or your website?
  - ▸ Be part of your Refer-a-Friend program?

Message

- Communicate talking points or ideas to your Buzz team.
- Try to strike the right balance between being organized versus overloading people with papers or emails, or pushing people to become your sales force.

Motivating your Buzz team

- Let them know how their efforts materialized and what the result was.
- Let them know about your overall successes and future plans. Keep them in the loop.
- Consider getting them a little gift.
- Try to find opportunities to WOM or network on *their* behalf.

Chapter Summary – *What you need to know*

- ☑ Most business owners begin marketing by asking friends, family and their personal network to spread the word about them.

- ☑ A Buzz team is a more structured and deliberate approach to proactively asking people to WOM on your behalf.

- ☑ Creating a Buzz teams means:
  - *Asking a lot more people if they will agree to talk about you to others.*
  - *Getting comfortable with people answering 'yes', but never following up, or even giving you a straight 'no'.*
  - *Setting clear expectations to members of the group.*
  - *Supplying them with the message and perhaps even the format (for example, writing an email for them that they can forward as if it was their own).*
  - *Motivating the team. Offering to WOM on their behalf is a great way to do that.*

- ☑ Creating a board of directors is one way many businesses achieve the goal of creating a buzz team.

Exercises

- ☑ Start small: Think of one or two people you can ask to WOM for you. Think about the right way to approach them. Is it a phone call, a meeting over coffee, an email? Remember that the more intimate the meeting or the relationship, the more comfortable and motivated would people be to WOM for you.

15 INFLUENCER MARKETING

The Big Idea

We all know people who are adept at influencing others. Reporters write stories or reviews that influence people's perceptions of events or products. Industry experts and consultants publish their thoughts online and offline. Bloggers offer their personal musings on a regular basis and are even considered reliable sources of knowledge. In business, an Influencer might be a decision-maker in a big company. There are also people who are icons in civil society. This group is harder to define, but it includes those who sit on various community boards, or who take some formal civic leadership role. More simply, anyone who knows a lot of people in a certain community and is often relied upon for advice on how to get stuff done is an Influencer ("The Influentials" a book by Jon Berry and Ed Keller was my first introduction to this concept). It is up to you to define who has an extra-ordinary ability to "teach" others about you. Influencers deserve extra attention because they represent a massive WOM opportunity.

Most of us know a handful of people who fit the Influencer profile. Figuring out what kind of Influencers are important for your business and how to reach them are the first steps in Influencer networking. Influencers must embody one or more of the four attributes of WOM facilitation we described in the WOM framework: *Social circle size, technical ability, credibility and motivation*. Let's start with the latter one. I believe that people with a smaller social circle, low technical ability and moderate credibility can more than compensate for those shortcomings with a high level of motivation. I am sure that, in the past, friends and family have gone that extra mile to ensure you achieve great results. Those who are already motivated comprise the first group of Influencers you should focus on. The trick, though, is to find a way to motivate the high-leverage Influencers you network with to WOM about you. This requires a combination of building the case for why WOMing about you will be beneficial to Influencers (or at least why it would make them look good), and making sure that they spread your message.

Two groups of Influencers are relevant to businesses: **Break-out Influencers** and **Local-presence Influencers**.

Break-out Influencers: A reporter who writes a story about you can function as an Influencer who helps you to 'break out'. Media and PR that publicizes your business is also included in this category. In the online world, the chances of capturing 'media' attention (including Bloggers or website writers) are higher. Why? Given the ballooning number of websites, an online bottleneck is created by a lack of exciting content. In other words, there is a lot of space and not enough good material. The more interesting and exciting your story, the greater the chance the interesting and exciting Blog entry will be about you. Another break-out opportunity is created when a corporate executive decides to hire you or buy from you.

Local-presence Influencers: I'll start close to home with this one. My wife Allie has a vast social network in our town, is involved in various community organizations and is a very active homeowner. My wife gets quite a few calls from friends and neighbors who are in the market for a new contractor, a doctor or even a cake decorator. People seek her advice and often follow it. She is a local-presence Influencer, and I am willing to bet that our contractors (and others) have made a handsome sum enjoying her WOM. What's in it for her? First, I think that she enjoys being helpful and appearing knowledgeable. That, and in my experience, professionals are willing to do an especially good job for her and respond quickly when she calls.

Using another example, a friend of mine launched a video editing business. He began work on a project with footage a client had provided of his recently deceased father. The edited video was well produced and the family really appreciated the memorial project. The son happened to be a fairly connected finance executive. He didn't have any more video editing projects, but he promised to give my friend's name to relevant people in his rolodex. These are examples of people on the local scene who can function as important Influencers for your business.

Can every business benefit from Influencer marketing? I believe so. It is probably worth a reasonable effort since it can greatly increase WOM. Does a business need Influencer support to launch or thrive? Not necessarily; I know of many businesses that built their reputation slowly and sequentially without any major WOM leaps forward.

What Big Corporations Do

For corporations, Influencers are a necessary evil. Companies like having their support, but asking for it means relinquishing control and opening themselves up to criticism and potentially negative WOM. The safest route for corporations seeking endorsement is to buy it. Popular options include celebrity endorsement, product placements in TV shows/movies, or creating ads where 'regular' folks describe their positive experience with the brand. Companies also try to get mentioned in mass media. Mass media meets 'Influencer' criteria: It reaches many people and is generally considered credible. For example, technology companies often offer new products to newspapers and websites for review. The Mossberg Solution Personal Technology column in the *Wall Street Journal* is probably one of the most widely read of its kind. Excerpts from Mossberg's column have even been quoted in advertisements. I am sure that corporate executives whose products are reviewed by Walter Mossberg read it with trembling hands. Sometimes, companies try to become influencers themselves by sending key executives for interviews. *Time* and *Newsweek* magazines sometimes offer a cover-page story to a company if they get dibs on covering the introduction of a hotly anticipated new product. A few examples are movies, Apple's iPhone and even the now almost-forgotten Segway.

Besides the 'big' players (media, celebrities), companies also try to find Influencers among their own customer base. Their rationale is that a WOM marketing program should not be targeted at everyone, but start with those most likely to spread the word. There is controversy in the WOM field about whether this is actually possible. Some companies suggest that a Myers-Briggs Type Indicator (MBTI) test can identify the most influential customers. The MBTI is a behavioral test that evaluates people's work and leadership styles. For example, a software company wants to give a select few of its customers a free trial of a hot new product. In return, they want positive WOM. In theory, an MBTI profile allows the company to focus first on its most influential customers, the ones it wishes to use as a starting point for a campaign.

The problem is that a person's propensity to be an Influencer does not necessarily mean that they are an Influencer in real life. Plus, as we mentioned before, they must have a reasonably big network, possess some technical ability, and, most importantly, be motivated to become a WOM spreader. Some companies argue that they can build statistical models that identify Influencers. I can see how that might be possible if a company married psychological or behavioral questionnaires with real performance data and basic surveys. For example, some companies take the fact that somebody is a repeat buyer as a signal that they will be motivated to WOM. A few simple survey questions, like how many people do you email in a regular week outside of work, or how many community groups are you involved with says something about their social circle. Another approach is simply to let people self select as Influencers: People who visit a section at the company website that encourages those who want to learn more or give feedback to respond. The idea is that customers who are so engaged with the brand that they agree to spend more time on it are more likely to be promoters, and, therefore, motivated to influence others.

Assuming that corporations can identify Influencers, there are several tactics they employ. Many offer membership in 'insider clubs' that allow members to be the first to experience and comment on new products or other developments. These clubs might also offer access to key company employees either directly or through Blogs and message boards. Companies often create live events for identified Influencers. Some invite them to HQ and some go on tour. Corporations hope that paying attention, including offering unique (and cool) products and information, to Influencers will encourage them to WOM.

Making It Happen

In the 'Big idea' section, we talked about two broad groups of Influencers: Break-out Influencers and Local-presence Influencers. Break-outs are those who can help a business leap forward in terms of exposure and WOM. Usually, their *job* is to be an Influencer. Examples include reporters, Bloggers, or senior decision makers at corporations. Local-presence Influencers are those who either have a vast social network, or are considered local hubs of information (the person everybody calls for advice). Broadly speaking, most people stumble across Local-presence Influencers as they get to know people in their communities, or as their client base increases. Break-out Influencers, however, are harder to reach and require a more deliberate plan.

Local-presence Influencers

Who are your Local-presence Influencers?

The best people to start with are those you already know, and perhaps have already worked with in the past. In fact, your best bet may be the people who are already spreading some positive Natural WOM about you, but you believe have the potential to reach more people. Next, you should try to identify targets that are not as familiar with you or your work. Can you network your way into introducing yourself? Can you let them sample your work or give them some free advice? As with every networking effort, creativity is paramount.

What would you like Influencers to WOM about?

In reality, you use the same tools to encourage a Local-presence Influencer to WOM about you as you would with any other prospect. The key difference is that, with an Influencer, you really want your efforts to succeed. As a result, you might spend more time involved in Two-way Conversations, or be more revealing about your story. Clearly, if they are your clients, not only you will want to perform at the highest standard, but make your business worth talking about.

Motivating them

Asking Influencers to WOM is your first tactic. Natural WOM is great, but encouraging people to WOM more positively and to more people can achieve incrementally better results. As I mentioned in the last few chapters, I believe that people inherently want to help out if asked, especially if they have a personal connection to the person asking, and when helping out does not require significant resources on their part.

Try to answer the 'what's in it for me?' question for your Influencers when you speak to them. Communicate to them that they have a valuable insider's viewpoint on your business, your plans and your story. Make them feel knowledgeable and give them a reason to share their information with others.

Also, mention any special deals or offers to them. Most importantly, do a great job for them whenever you get the chance. If you are considered a 'great find' in their books, they will be proud to tell their contacts about you.

Feedback loop (to them and to yourself)

Your Influencers will want to know if their WOM activities work. Assure them that they are indeed Influencers by telling them that their contacts have reached out to you. Also, asking "how did you hear about us" (the basic WOM assessment question) also helps you identify any Influencers who are currently driving business, or even identify new Influencers you were previously unaware of.

Break-out Influencer

Who are your potential Break-out Influencers?

Every business can benefit from public relations: An article in a local paper, an interview on a radio show, or even a mention at a Blog site. Many businesses never receive media attention and are doing just fine. Others, however, certainly benefit from exposure: Businesses that have a unique product or service, those that sell products directly to consumers, or those that sell advice or consulting. There may be other categories. Try this exercise to see if there is something here for you: Imagine that your local paper offers you the chance to write a story for the front page of the business section about yourself. Would you have something to write about that is both interesting and will make a difference to your bottom line in some way (for example, something that will raise awareness of your business)? If the answer is yes, you might want to think more about how to get media attention.

If you are selling to bigger companies or entities (e.g. government agencies), you don't need me to tell you who the Influencers are: They are the decision makers and their advisors. One thing to note is that even if you are mostly focused on consumers or smaller companies, winning over a bigger client can give a tremendous boost to your credibility. You can cash in on that credibility by creating testimonials or case studies highlighting bigger clients. This kind of information sharing is a great way to begin or support WOM campaigns (see Chapter 11 on information sharing).

Reaching Break-out Influencers

Reaching out to this group is hard work. Get ready for rejections or simply being ignored. The best approach is to try to network your way to these high-leverage individuals. Use your personal network to find people who know members of your target Influencer group. If that doesn't work and you have to begin 'cold calling', make sure that you follow WOM and networking best practices: Be sure to highlight what's unique and conversation worthy about you. Start by picking up the phone. If you get an answering machine, tell him/her that you will follow up with an email. Send them some information about you by email, or even snail mail. Remain positive, enthusiastic and, most importantly, persistent. Call or email after some time to inquire if the person has had a chance to look over your information. When you get a chance to talk to the person or begin an email exchange, make it clear what you expect them to do (write about you in their Blog or newspaper, schedule a demonstration, talk to others in their network, and so on).

Chapter Summary – *What you need to know*

☑ Influencers are people who have an above-average ability to spread WOM.

☑ They must rate highly on one of the WOM facilitating attributes:

- *Large social circle size (e.g. they can talk to or send email to many others).*
- *Technical ability (e.g. they use email frequently, write a Blog etc).*
- *Credibility (We are all experts in something; some are considered to be more of an authority in some areas).*
- *Motivation (The most important attribute; those who are willing to go above and beyond to support a cause can sometimes achieve surprising results).*

☑ We identify two kinds of Influencers

- *Break-out influencers: Reporters, bloggers, decision makers with important potential clients.*
- *Local-presence influencers: A loosely defined group that includes those that are either very involved in the local community or are commonly called for their advice on various ideas or purchase decisions. Again, they are hard to define, but when you meet one, you know it.*

☑ Each one of the Influencer groups requires a unique strategy to motivate them to WOM for you.

- *A key question to answer in every case is: What's in it for them if they WOM?*

Exercises

☑ Create a short list of Influencers you would like reach. Talk to people in your personal network; who do they think is an important influencer for you?

16 REFER A FRIEND

The Big Idea

A Refer-a-friend program is a form of WOM marketing that includes an incentive. The simple Refer-a-friend (RAF) model should sound familiar. For example, when a customer refers a family member who purchases a product, the person referring receives some type of reward. Many businesses opt for a RAF model because it's usually fairly easy to implement, requires minimal strategic planning, and can actually be quite effective. I believe that there is untapped value in RAF. Progressive businesses can and should create revamped RAF programs in support of their efforts to build an engine powering continuous growth.

What Big Corporations Do

Most companies use a simple system: Refer a friend to us and you will receive a gift (cash, gift card, a book). The first company to break that mold back in 1992 was MCI with their 'Friends and Family' calling program. The plan went through various incarnations, but the basic premise was this: You chose 20 people to include in your plan and you got a 20 percent discount when you called them. The catch was that they also had to be MCI customers. At the time, this was ground breaking. The result was that MCI customers were asking their friends to join the MCI calling plans. Not only was the person making the referral getting a gift, but the person being referred gets one as well (because they also got discounted calls). Plus, the connection between the two customers and the constant reward (in the form of a discount) encouraged further loyalty. After all, "if we both get 20 percent off every time we talk, why leave the plan?" The plan was tremendously successful and the company received marketing industry awards, including the American Marketing Association's top innovation award.

Companies today use various methods to inject new life into Refer-a-friend programs. Take video or mobile games companies, for example. Several of them have created programs that reward people for encouraging others to join in a game. From a marketing perspective, there is a very big difference between, "do this, I did it too," which is essentially what we say when we refer people to most consumer products, and "join me in the game." Like the MCI program, both parties share an experience, in this case a game they can play together and continue to discuss online and offline. Greater interaction between people and the product usually produces greater levels of loyalty, and possibly more referrals.

Even simple Refer-a-friend programs work. If they didn't, banks wouldn't continue to shower new customers and those who refer to them with gifts ranging from MP3 players to grills. RAFs are easy to experiment with in a test and control fashion, so I am confident that at least some banks verified their profitability. Considering the high return on a long-term banking customer, gifts seem a worthwhile investment. The current status quo in banking is to give a higher perception, but lower-value gift, and change the gift every few months to keep the promotion fresh. Sounds simple and it seems to work.

Making It Happen

Rewards and incentives are a very established way to acquire new customers and keep them loyal. I am confident that many readers are members of some form of rewards program. RAF programs essentially reward people for being part of a network they can tap into and motivate. Rewards can be given to one or both people in this interaction. There is a fine line, though, between enticing people to promote a product in exchange for a fun reward, and remunerating them for becoming salesmen or saleswomen.

The success of an RAF program depends on the same factors at play in other product launches. You need to nail down your market's attitude towards the program using market research. It could be that a simple discount for the person referring is all you require. Once you come up with your concept, be sure to test and modify accordingly. Below are some of the steps you need to consider when developing your Refer-a-friend plan.

Develop an idea
Key insight #1: It's not just about the money.

When a person refers a friend, they want to feel that they are giving good advice about a new product or service. Never mind that the impetus to tell another person about it was a reward; friends and confidence in the product come first. Rewards only create a gentle push. Understanding a customer's priorities in this regard can help marketers generate ideas about how to break the 'Refer-a-friend-for-a-gift-certificate' mold.

The first thing to consider is how a RAF program might enhance the relationship between the customer and the person being referred. For example, the reward might be a lunch for two. Any activity that can be shared by both parties achieves the 'relationship first' principle in RAF (sending them to a movie, giving them access to an online subscription, and so on). Plus, to maintain loyalty, you can arrange that more rewards will be bestowed occasionally in the future.

Next, focus on the product itself. Do you have or can you create products that are available by invitation only? In other words, can you offer something unique or exclusive? Are there other ways you can modify your product to a RAF program to encourage referrals? The execution of such a strategy can be as simple as offering a discount only to those who come in as referrals.

Finally, what kinds of rewards do people appreciate? I believe that the best rewards are WOM-worthy by themselves. Offering a unique, cool, fun, or even bizarre reward that catches people's attention will accomplish this. But again, a simple gift card might work just fine. Like the bank programs I mentioned, you want the reward to have high perceived value and low(er) actual cost. You will also want to change the reward once in a while, unless it really works well. Consider trying an escalating reward: The more people a customer brings in, the more they receive for *each* referral. Another option is to extend the reward to a third entity, for example a charity all parties feel strongly about. This strategy becomes even more powerful if the charity is somehow connected to what your company does.

Find your target market

Key Insight #2: Neutrals to your company can be turned into Promoters of the RAF program.

It seems logical to argue that only Promoters or Evangelists of your company will react positively to a RAF program. If people are Neutral (usually the biggest group) about a company, can they be turned into Promoters through an RAF program? I believe this is possible. In a RAF program, you want people to promote *it* as well as your product. If the RAF program gets people excited, whether it's the incentive, the unique offer, or the way the offer makes referees feel, it will work well with Neutrals. Put differently, a well-designed RAF can convert people who usually feel Neutral about your company into promoters of the RAF.

Do your market research

Key insight #3: Walk in your customers' shoes.

Once you have several ideas for an RAF and a basic understanding of your target market, it is time to do some market research. Starting an RAF program is a big move for any business, so gaining as much intelligence as you can before the launch just makes sense. The way most businesses do this is by incorporating it into their daily conversations: "I am thinking about starting an RAF program that would be special because....What do you think?" By the way, this is how big corporations vet their ideas. The only difference is that bigger companies usually find it harder to gain access to customers or potential customers. Instead, they turn to things like focus groups or one-on-one interviews.

You must act on your research by making any necessary changes to your RAF plan. Marketers are often surprised at how the best ideas look very different in the eyes of their customers. With any luck, feedback to your ideas will translate into slight modifications, not a 'wreck and rebuild' operation.

Test your RAF

Key insight #4: You don't have to offer RAF to everybody at the outset.

It is better to put your toe in the water before you make the RAF program a permanent part your business. Smaller businesses will find it harder to do testing, but it is a concept definitely worth thinking about.

Test your way into RAF:

- Only promote it via certain channels (only in letters you send, advertise it exclusively on your website, or make it available just to people you talk to personally).
- Offer it for a limited time period.
- Offer it only in a certain geographical area (relevant for bigger businesses).

Consider the effect of gamers

Key insight #5: Gamers (those who try to work the system to maximize benefits) usually don't pose a huge problem if the reward/compensation is reasonable.

In a great RAF program, the incentive is only part of the reason to refer. In cases where the RAF incentive is very high, people might try to "game" the system just to get the reward. For example, if a daycare center offers an iPod to every current customer who refers a friend, I can envision a situation where parents new to a neighborhood might try to "partner" with a current customer to ensure they also get an iPod out of the deal. When people really believe in you and your product, and your RAF program is about building relationships and not just giving out cash, gamers should pose a minor nuisance, not more.

Final thought: Some corporate RAF programs limit the number of referrals allowed per person in a period of time. I find it hard to believe this would be an issue for many businesses, but it is worth considering.

Create an easy-to-use program

Key insight #6: Make it easy.

Did I say easy? RAF programs should take no more than a couple of sentences to explain. Referring should be easy and getting compensation should be close to automatic.

Things you need to consider:

- Explaining the offer (and the process):
  - How do you explain it in person?
  - How do you present it on your website/brochure?
- Easy to remember where to find RAF details:
  - When people hear about a RAF program for the first time, they may not yet have a potential referral in mind. When they do find

someone they want to refer, it should be easy for them to find details. For example, you can tell them in advance that details appear on your website or that they can email you.

- Making it easy to refer:
  - ▸ Create an easy-to-explain RAF plan.
  - ▸ Send it out and tell people to keep handy: Letter, email, website, freebie, brochure or any other material you plan to leave with your contacts.
  - ▸ Share advice on how to sell to others: For example, testimonials about how others had success referring.
  - ▸ Make sure it is clear how you will identify the original referrer. For example, should that referrer give a certain code to those they refer or just their name?
- Distributing the rewards:
  - ▸ Regardless of who receives the rewards (referrer, friend, both, or a third party), make sure they are delivered in a reasonable time frame.

Capture information and analyze

Implement a simple system to register RAF details. You will need that anyway for reward fulfillment, but you should also use it to analyze the program and see if it is working for you. Also, when you get a chance to talk to the referring person or the friend, it is always a good idea to try to solicit some feedback from them about the program. In fact, this is a great way to start a Two-way Conversation.

Chapter Summary – *What you need to know*

☑ A Refer-a-friend program is a form of WOM marketing that includes an incentive directed at the person referring new business to you.

☑ Refer-a-friend programs can be as simple as offering a gift certificate to the person referring; however, breaking the mold by coming up with original program designs can be a lot more effective.

☑ We covered six key insights in the chapter:

- *It's not just about the money.*
  - *Relationship building can be as important (or more) for referrers than the incentive.*
  - *Incentives that enhance the relationship (for example, both parties get a prize, or exclusive 'invitation only' rewards) can be especially effective.*
- *Neutrals to your company can be turned into Promoters of the RAF program.*
  - *It is likely that a well-design RAF will get people more excited than they otherwise might be about you and your company.*
- *Walk in your customers' shoes.*
  - *Do some market research before you launch; float your ideas past customers and friends to see what they think.*
- *You don't have to offer RAF to everybody at the outset.*
  - *In fact, it might be better to test your way into a program.*
- *Gamers (those who try to work the system to maximize benefits) usually don't pose a huge problem if the reward/compensation is reasonable.*
- *Make it easy*
  - *A great RAF program is easy to explain, makes it easy to refer and easy to redeem the prize or incentive*

SECTION III

Enabling WOM

17 INTRO TO CONVERSION

You have deployed a variety of WOM marketing tactics. People are motivated to talk about your business to friends, family and colleagues. They are making positive comments. Your WOM marketing is achieving its initial goals; now let's focus on the person receiving the comment or story. A person hearing WOM can react in any one of four ways:

- **Not Interested**: In a worse-case scenario, lack of interest isn't that bad an outcome. Companies small and big invest huge sums in advertising and direct marketing, and not everybody becomes a new client. In fact, many don't even remember the advertisement. Post-WOM, you should assume that there will be a **conversion ratio**. No formal study has confirmed this, but I believe that the sales conversion rate of positive WOM is several folds higher than any other form of non-personal advertising or direct marketing. Getting somebody to independently say something positive about you is more powerful than any ad.
There are numerous reasons why people may not take any action. Perhaps they are not in the market for the product and won't be in the near future. They may perceive the source as not credible, and though the comment may be positive, they are just not persuaded. Even though the story you start with might be conversation-worthy, it might not be memorable to the receiver.

- **Awareness**: Some conversations do make it into our memory bank. We remember something about the comments, how positive they were and who delivered them. We may draw on these conversations when we begin thinking about making a purchase. In marketing-speak, this is called 'awareness building'. If somebody isn't aware you exist, they definitely won't consider you while researching various purchasing options. When somebody talks about you, the minimum you have achieved is awareness. For businesses, that's a lot! Big corporations can make the call that they want a certain segment of the population to know about a new product launch. Given enough marketing dollars, I can almost guarantee that more than 50 percent of their target market will, in a fairly short period of time, know about the new product. Smaller businesses don't have that kind of money and, as we mentioned at the outset, many don't do any advertising at all.

- **Consideration/inquiry**: When somebody is at the consideration stage, they are thinking about buying something, but haven't decided exactly what they want to get and from whom. In this phase, they often seek advice from others. Your goal should be to create an opportunity for them to hear from somebody who is part of your WOM marketing campaign (or to ensure that such a conversation happened in the past). Assuming that this conversation takes place, the potential buyer may decide to consider your business, or at least inquire about you. When a person decides to 'check you out', it must be extremely easy to find you. As we discussed in previous chapters, it's important your WOM campaign includes information on how to locate you. In the 'Availability' chapter (next chapter), we outline the various ways you can make it easy to find you, even if all people know about you is your name.

- **A new purchase is made**: I include two outcomes in this category:
  - ① A new customer is acquired.
  - ② A customer who currently uses a service (e.g. gets yard maintenance) or who makes recurring purchases (goes to a hairdresser) becomes more loyal.

Are WOM comments enough to persuade someone to immediately buy from you? Clearly they are. Think about your recent purchases (excluding those things you buy regularly). I am sure you will find several examples of things you bought as a direct result of WOM. In a similar fashion, I am sure you can recall sharing your thoughts about something you already bought with others. If they came away with a similarly good impression of the product, don't you feel more loyal?

- **Relays the message forward**. Regardless if the person decides to follow up on a conversation or not, another great outcome might be that they continue to move the information they received forward. A successful WOM marketing campaign will have '**Progressive Waves of WOM**'. Progressive Waves will happen naturally with the right stories. If your story is cool and conversation worthy, people will talk about it. In fact, if your story makes it through the first round of WOM (somebody starts spreading it), it is likely to continue spreading. Some businesses (especially Internet-based) desire to reach the 'Tipping Point', the term Malcolm Gladwell coined for a situation where these Progressive Waves are so strong that everybody is talking about a certain product, making it massively popular. However, businesses usually don't expect their stories to become huge success stories. In most cases, their goals are a lot less ambitious and more localized. Nevertheless, you can expect progressive waves of WOM to happen, and it is very satisfying when they do.

Chapter Summary – *What you need to know*

☑ In this chapter, we focused on the person who receives stories or information about you or your business from others (the recipients of WOM).

- *There are five possible outcomes when they hear something about you:*
  - *Not interested*
  - *Awareness*
  - *Consideration/inquiry*
  - *A new purchase made*
  - *Relays the message forward*

18 AVAILABILITY– MAKE IT EASY TO FIND YOU

People have heard positive things about you and they want to follow up. Your next challenge is to make sure that when people look for your business, they can find you. The problem is that in many conversations about your business, contact information is not passed along. On the receiving end, in some cases the only thing people will remember about you is your name or business name. There are several steps you can take to increase your chances of being found.

There are essentially two possible WOM scenarios in which your contact info will be provided to potential customers:

Scenario One:
Contact information is a passed on in the original WOM conversation (by referring person).

> ▸ *For example*: Two friends are talking about graphic design. When one of the friends recommends a specific graphic designer, she immediately forwards the designer's email address.

Scenario Two:
People start looking for you days or months post the initial WOM conversation.

> ▸ *For example*: A person searching for a graphic designer thinks about a conversation he had a week ago in which the name of a specific designer was mentioned. He finds her name online and gives her a call.

To cover all your bases, you really need to make sure that in each scenario, chances are high that those searching for you will find you easily.

Scenario One: Contact info is included in the
WOM conversation (by referring person)

The best outcome occurs when contact information is passed on by the referring person within the original conversation, eliminating the need for any extra steps. To make sure this happens, it is imperative you leave something that includes your information with people you interact with. They can refer to it when they are WOMing.

Depending on whether the WOM conversation is Natural WOM or Amplified WOM affects how information is passed. We defined Natural WOM in the first section as conversations that are a result of the normal course of business, not part of a specific WOM campaign. Your business, your product and the way you interact with your customers is already a topic of conversation for some people. We also said that Amplified WOM happens when marketers try to encourage more people to make more positive comments about a product or service. There is no clear distinction between Natural and Amplified WOM, but in the context of 'being available', there are some important differences. In an Amplified WOM marketing effort, your contact information will be embedded in the referring effort. For example, if the goal of an Amplified WOM campaign is for people to pass emails along, your info is already included. In contrast, if somebody tells the story of how you started your business (Natural WOM), it may not be immediately obvious that the person telling the story has access to your contact information. Making sure they do and can easily share it is an important goal for businesses seeking referrals.

Your goal in a Natural WOM conversation is that the person making the recommendation will have easy access to your contact info and share it with the new prospect.

Make it easy for the *person referring* to get access to your contact info:
- A business card (give them a few).
- A brochure (leave with them at least one).
- A prominent location that is easy to remember or give directions to (directions to either your actual business or a sign of your business with more details).
  - ▶ *Example 1: You have a store in a well-known location.*
  - ▶ *Example 2: You have a prominent ad in the Yellow Pages.*
  - ▶ *Example 3: You have a permanent sign in an area motorists drive through.*
- A catchy, easy-to-remember website address or 1-800.
- An email that can be forwarded.
- A freebie reminder: Fridge magnet, bookmark, pen (give them a few).

These 'reminders' serve dual functions. They allow a referring person to easily direct their audience to the business they are recommending. They also serve as reminders to call you again for repeat business.

**Scenario two: People start looking for you days
or months post the initial WOM conversation**

Someone may hear positive things about you, but don't need or want to follow up at that time. A few weeks or months may pass before they decide it is time to find you. It's important that you make sure their search will be quick and fruitful.

When people search for you, they may already have a very good sense of who you are and how to find you. However, they may only remember your name or what you do. For example, I may be advised to try a new Cajun restaurant in my city. I may remember the name of the place a few weeks later, but if I don't, I will probably look under the more generic term 'Cajun restaurant' and hope the search results will refresh my memory. You need a plan to ensure that a simple search for you – by name or by profession/industry/specialty – will yield results quickly.

How are people likely to search for you?

Think about the profiles of the people seeking you out. How are they likely to search for you (online, looking for your shop in a mall, newspapers ads, classifieds, Yellow Pages)? Think about what they are going to be looking for. For example, they may be searching for your name specifically. However, as mentioned above, if they have forgotten your name, their search will be more generic. What are some likely avenues they might take? Map out the possible ways people will search for you.

Assessing your availability

To assess how easy it is to find you, you will need to walk in your customers' shoes and search for your business yourself. To keep yourself honest and create a comprehensive 'to do' list, ask others to look for you in various ways and see what they find.

Searching for you **Online:**

- Search Engines (Google, Yahoo, MSN and Ask)
  - ▸ Find you by name
  - ▸ Find you with more generic terms
  - ▸ Find you by the problem you solve or your product
  - ▸ Find you with the name of your area in the search term
- Search Engines (local edition)
  - ▸ Google Local, Yahoo Local
- Other consolidating websites
  - ▸ Your city's or area's sites (e.g. Richmond.com)
  - ▸ Your industry's website
  - ▸ Online Yellow Pages (e.g. Verizon SuperPages)

Searching for you **Offline**
- Yellow Pages
  - ▸ Some businesses consider different categories for the same business
- Search for your sign in your area
- Classified or other newspaper advertising

Chapter Summary – *What you need to know*

☑ After people hear about you, hopefully some of them will decide to look for you. It is imperative that you make finding you easy and fast.

☑ There are two scenarios that you need to plan for:
- *When information about finding you was passed in the initial WOM conversation.*
- *When somebody decides to look for you several days or weeks after the WOM interaction (and have limited data about you).*

Exercises

☑ Search for yourself under both scenarios as detailed at the end of this chapter.
- *Make sure to let others search for you. Different people look for things differently.*

MEASURING RESULTS

WOM marketing is a challenge to measure. It's difficult to find out who is talking, on what topics and how often. It is even harder to know whether the message is registering with listeners and converting them into customers. With those challenges in mind, it is worthwhile to think about what *can* be measured.

How did you hear about us?

If you are going to use only one measurement method, this is the one you should start with. Even if you are not doing any Amplified WOM marketing, it is crucial to know how your other marketing efforts work, including Natural WOM. A couple of things to keep in mind:

① **Keep some statistics, if possible**. You need to have a clear set of answers on record. In other words, people might describe how they heard about you in various ways, but you need to have about ten options for how to record their responses. This is especially important when the question is asked by one of your employees (helps with consistency).

② **Ask early**. Educate whoever is talking to new or returning customers to ask that question at some point in the initial conversation. Asking later might mean that they will forget how they heard about you. Make it part of your routine.

③ **Dive deeper, if possible.** If you can form a relationship with the person contacting you, you can expand your inquiry. For example, what did they hear about you and from *whom*? Did they also contact your competitors?

Feeling comfortable with anecdotal evidence

Business people and SB owners, in particular, often need to make decisions based on few data points. In the WOM marketing space, you may not have a chance to engage in multiple conversations that will lead to analysis based on 'hard data'. That should not diminish the importance of the information you get. Big businesses often rely on anecdotal evidence to make important decisions. For example, when launching a new product, corporations will perform focus groups with usually no more than eight people in each, or they will follow consumers home to see how they actually use the product. A couple of negative comments in those forums can sink a multi-million dollar product idea. I have been to many focus groups and individual interviews, and what I've learned is that, very quickly, two or three major themes emerge. If people don't like a product or a marketing message for a particular reason, you will hear that reason again and again in almost every group. This might seem somewhat counterintuitive; after all, people and their life experiences are so diverse. The bottom line is that we are more similar to each other than we might expect. This is good news for businesses: As long as you know that the population you are talking to is not skewed in a certain direction (e. g. talking to a crowd that is younger or older than your average customer, or talking only to your family and friends), if you hear the same feedback again and again, you can feel safe believing it.

Get feedback from those you interact with

Start with people you feel more comfortable talking to, like your personal network. Then, try to expand to your buzz team to people you have offered the Refer A Friend program to, and even to other customers you have been in contact with in the past. Try to get some feedback on your WOM marketing tactics as well.

The best way to start a conversation is to begin with some general questions about your business (feedback on your products or service, or on a new idea you have, etc). Then, if you feel comfortable, try to probe whether people have been talking to others about you. Can they remember what they talked about and to whom? If you can make connections between these conversations and actual sales you've made, even better.

Use a third party to ask questions on your behalf

Some people may not feel comfortable giving their opinions about your business in a one-on-one setting. From their perspective, face-to-face feedback is hard to do and can feel awkward if there is no existing relationship. If you can ask people in your network to pose questions on your behalf, you are bound to get more 'juicy', relevant information about what's working and what's not in your WOM marketing campaign. In fact, this form of market research can teach you a lot about your business as a whole.

Scan online resources

Depending on your business, people might be writing about you in Blogs or message boards (though this is probably relevant to a small minority of readers of this book). However, as online media gains in popularity, keep an eye on them.

Take action

Measurement is only important if it's actionable. Embrace positive and negative feedback, and make the necessary changes when you feel that you have enough data to make a call.

Chapter Summary – *What you need to know*

☑ WOM is hard to measure, but you can definitely gain some intelligence about what's working.

☑ The two key questions to ask every new prospect are:
- *How did you hear about us?*
- *What did you hear about us?*

☑ You should ask people you feel more comfortable with about their opinions, as well as asking others to ask customers (or prospects) questions on your behalf.

☑ Feeling comfortable with anecdotal evidence is a key skill to develop.

☑ Think clearly about what feels like a one-off comment and what feels like a relevant finding. Then, take action to become more effective.

Exercises

☑ Start keeping a log of people's answers to the two key questions above. After getting about ten answers, assess what these answers mean to you.
- *For example, is somebody in the community referring a lot of work to you? Has any of your advertising actually influenced them?*

About half of businesses use only WOM marketing and don't invest in other forms of marketing or advertising. The other half uses a mix of traditional advertising and some reliance on WOM to develop their business. For those who plan to continue to rely *only* on WOM marketing, there are some investment issues they need to consider. Investment in WOM marketing is not free. Even if no actual dollars are spent, time is money. As a result, experimentation is a great way to find out what works and what doesn't before making a major investment. For businesses that do consider paid advertising, WOM marketing can support advertising efforts to achieve better results. Similarly, more traditional advertising can support and enhance current WOM marketing, and should be considered.

WOM in the marketing mix principles:

- **WOM is just one marketing tactic**
  I believe that every business is affected by Natural WOM; but I am not sure that every business needs to have an explicit Amplified WOM strategy. Many businesses can develop solely focusing on direct mail or image advertising. WOM, just like every other investment decision, needs to be evaluated against a broad set of other marketing opportunities.

- **WOM marketing is not free**
  WOM marketing efforts are not free, even if there isn't an actual dollar investment. Your time can be spent doing 'billable' work. Alternatively, you can use your time for leisure. To that effect, WOM marketing should be prioritized along with other marketing options and other uses for your time. Engaging in Two-way Conversations or trying to build your Buzz group all takes time, time that could be spent just making cold calls or finishing up paper work, or even going home early. What's the best

use of your time?

Economic theory addresses the concept of diminishing returns. The idea is that when you try to improve something, you first identify the high-leverage action that you can take. At some point, putting more effort into improvement is going to give you less return than some of the initial actions. I am confident that when you read this book, you will begin to develop a hypothesis about which of the tactics can potentially work for you. Make sure that you prioritize accordingly. Some ideas make sense on paper, but if you feel like more effort is not actually getting you further ahead, stop. You may have reached a point of diminishing returns, where more WOM or other marketing endeavors are just not worth it any more.

- **Experiment, if possible**

  There are several tactics described in this book that can be tested on a small scale without a massive effort. Essentially, most tests focus on two outcomes:

  ① How easy is it to implement this test (and later the strategy as a whole)?

  ② What will be the results?

Most people have heard that it's important to maximize Return-on-investment (ROI). In this case, if you are going to employ a tactic that is hard to implement for your business, you should aim to get great results. Otherwise, a simpler effort with modest results might actually be a better use of your time. Because it's hard to say in advance how much work will go into each effort, and even harder to know what will work and what won't, it's important to test your way into new ideas before rolling out a strategy.

Let's look at a few examples:

WOM Marketing Tactic	How you can test your way into it
Refer a Friend	Offer the program to a select group of people (e.g. only 30 customers)
Creating a Reference/ Recommendation program	Observe the effect of giving access to references on only few potential buyers
Viral marketing	Create two (or more) versions of an email you want to people to forward and assess which works better
Two-way Conversations (TWC)	Try various ways to approach TWC (what you ask, how you pitch WOM, etc) and see which seems to make the other person more at ease to WOM on your behalf

- **WOM can support other advertising efforts**

  If you are part of the 55 percent of businesses that advertise, it's important to think about how your WOM marketing can support your other advertising (print, radio, outdoor signs, Yellow Pages).

▸ Align your WOM marketing with other forms of advertising

If you have an advertising campaign going on right now, you have already taken a few steps. You did some market research about your target audience. You know something about their attitudes (likes and dislikes), and you also know something about their media consumption habits. You surveyed the various media options (radio, newspaper, outdoor) and zeroed in on the best target given your budget. WOM marketing should support the same goals you identified when you decided to begin advertising. Your target market should be the same. The things you hype in a non-WOM marketing campaign can be a great start when planning WOM marketing (especially when you think about what about you is conversation worthy). Finally, the results from both can and should be measured and analyzed as much as possible.

▸ Build buzz into your actual marketing

We discussed in the 'Building WOM into your product' section how to create a product that has some conversation-worthy elements in it (those that can lead to WOM). Advertising can also be conversation worthy. For example, place a catchy sign in a unique location that gives people pause to wonder who put it there. You can imagine how radio ads and print ads reach similar goals. It is definitely not easy to get people's attention using any form of media, and make the message so memorable they will think about it *and* talk to their friends. It's challenging, but possible. Try to remember the last time somebody told you about an ad (I am sure it wasn't that long ago). As with any marketing effort, the key is to really understand your target audience, to speak their language, and engage them in a way that is unique and that captures their imagination.

- **WOM marketing can be supported by other marketing efforts**
  If there is something conversation-worthy about who you are or what you do, there might be a case to invest in actual advertising (if you have only relied on WOM marketing to date). Researching and developing a WOM marketing campaign is great preparation for a regular advertising campaign. Non-WOM marketing tends to focus on the company or its product, as opposed to the customer. If you are able to identify what people say about you or even encourage more positive conversations about you, you might also be able to create superb (more traditional) marketing materials that will further support those conversations.

Let's look at several example of how advertising can support WOM efforts:

WOM Marketing Tactics	Sample Advertising Copy
Reputation: great products and services	People are already talking about our new Widget functionality, allow us to clarify...
Your story, your first step	We had our ups and downs, but there is a happy ending...
WOM built into your business (Natural WOM)	We heard that we are the only widget maker that has...
Two-way Conversations (TWC)	Dear widget user: Thank you for partnering with us. Can you take a few minutes to tell us about how we can serve your community better? Go online to survey.com ...
Information sharing and product experience for WOM	We do house calls. Send us an email, we will organize a test drive.
Creating a Reference/ Recommendation program	We have more than 20 customers willing to receive your call to tell you more about us. Can your current widget provider do that?
Viral Marketing	Know anybody that cares about widgets? Our site has the most up-to-date report for you to forward.
Influencer marketing	Mr. X and Company Y are using our widget. Want to know why?
Refer-a-friend	Do you know any of our customers? They have 20 percent discount certificates to give out...
Availability - make it easy to find you	Check out our new website at easy-to-remember-address.com

Chapter Summary – *What you need to know*

☑ WOM is just one marketing tactic
- *Great businesses can be built with just natural WOM and/or advertising. Amplified WOM is just one tactic out of many.*

☑ WOM marketing is not free
- *Time is money. Investing your efforts in WOM marketing happens at the expense of other business or personal endeavors.*

☑ Experiment, if possible
- *There are many ways to test your way into various WOM marketing techniques. No need to commit yourself early.*

☑ WOM can support other advertising efforts
- *Use what you learned about your target market in your preparation to begin advertising as you plan WOM marketing. Also, think about creating ads that are WOM-worthy.*

☑ WOM marketing can be supported by other marketing efforts
- *Things that work well in your WOM marketing can lead to very effective advertising using the same elements (see the table above for examples).*

21 NEGATIVE WOM

In section I, we defined Negative WOM as follows:

Negative comments may have the most impact of any WOM comments about your business. If people have a complaint about your business or service, they are more likely to complain to others than to you. Your ability to identify what upsets people about your product or service will allow you diminish the domino effect of negative WOM. Positive WOM can gradually build a business; negative WOM can quickly sink it. Businesses cannot afford negative WOM blind spots and need to devise strategies to "search and destroy" problems continuously.

Here are a couple of best practices regarding Negative WOM:

- **Be open to criticism**
  It is very hard to embrace negative feedback. We all know it presents an opportunity, but it is still difficult to take. Some businesses know that they have a long way to go before they can fix their problems; but many businesses just don't want to know. The thing that is deceiving about Negative WOM is that a business can remain successful in the face of it. If a business is achieving its numbers, why bother worrying about those who are dissatisfied? Even if the business is currently moving at a good pace, a new or existing player can come along at any point and take advantage of your weaknesses.

- **Understand the trade offs you make**
  Business requires compromise. Companies large and small continuously have to decide how much bang they will receive for their buck on various business functions (e.g. the level of customer service, product quality, and price). People will always want more, and it is human nature

to complain. In other words, some Negative WOM is just part of doing business. When you make conscious decisions about the trade offs you are making, and you are aware of and feel comfortable with the implications of your decisions, you are in control. If you are not sure that you understand the implications of a decision, take time to reconsider. For example, is the potential Negative WOM you will get by cutting costs worth it?

- **Be aware of blind spots**
  Imagine that you are doing things 80 percent right, but customers also mention the 20 percent you get wrong when they talk about you. It might not be enough for people to *not* recommend you, but it clearly sets you back. It's a blind spot. It could be anything – the way you make your sales pitch, your timeliness, even your logo. Blind spots are especially hard to identify because they are not necessarily 'deal killers'. However, addressing them is an important exercise in self awareness and shows maturity.
- **An action plan starts with research**

By yourself:

Disclaimer. Asking people for constructive criticism is not easy. It is also likely that people will not give it to you. Nevertheless, the more you can do, the better.

Two-way Conversations: As we mentioned in the TWC section (Chapter 9), asking people for feedback is going to make them feel more supportive of your business and of you, regardless if they actually tell you everything they think. In other words, asking for feedback always has an upside. When we talk about Negative Feedback, we are actually aiming to get actionable information from the conversation. This is made easier by:

- Starting with people who are closer to you and may feel more comfortable talking to you about this topic.
- Beginning the conversation with something that you already know to get things going: "A few people told me that…did you see/feel that as well?"
- Making it anonymous. While this is not in the spirit of Two-way Conversations, it still might be useful. This would not be relevant for people who have very few clients (it's not hard to guess where the feedback came from). There are various ways to perform an anonymous survey: A form that can be submitted in a special box that is opened once a month, an email with a survey/some questions in it. Make it happen before they leave and your relationship is temporarily over. Once they are gone, it's harder to make people fill in a form or answer an email survey. Instead, make it part of the process.

Using a Third Party:

Even the smallest of businesses can ask others for help in getting feedback. We discuss this at length in the Measurement chapter.

- **Don't take action on every comment**

I have been to many focus groups where customers had a chance to talk about product ideas. Occasionally, someone would describe a multi-feature product that was both high quality and low priced (or even free). That's, of course, impossible. As a whole, most people were demanding yet reasonable about what they expected from a company or a product. The same goes for the feedback you receive. Some of it is going to sound harsh, or even irrational. Don't sweat it, ignore it. In most cases, these comments will be few and far between.

- **Take reasonable action**
  In your business life, there are going to be 'a-ha' moments that require a complete re-thinking of the way you approach things; but there won't be many of them. In that spirit, take negative feedback in stride and think clearly about the possible outcomes of taking action. Consider the return you will get on your investment if you make changes. Having a better product or more attentive service has a clear dollar impact; as a result, continue to evaluate the cost/benefit effects of any move. Take your time before making a decision, if possible.

- **What to do with the Hostile segment**
  When we described the Endorsement spectrum in the first section, we described the Hostile group as individuals who are so angry at you that they are planning to take action to hurt your business. The damage that they can inflict is hard to predict. If you are able to read early warning signs indicating somebody is about to join the Hostile group, try to take reasonable action quickly. Get involved personally and promise to make things better, or at least compensate for any mistakes you might have made. Consider it an investment. In most cases, however, there will be no early warning and you will wake up one morning to bad news about you. This can come in the form of a website, a message board comment, an email or a newspaper article. If that happens, the only thing that you can do is to try to contact the Hostile person and correct the problem. Try to follow the concept of the Two-way Conversation: Listen first, suggest action later.

Chapter Summary – *What you need to know*

☑ Positive WOM can gradually build a business; negative WOM can quickly sink it.

☑ Businesses cannot afford any negative WOM blind spots and need to devise strategies to "search and destroy" problems continuously.

☑ To achieve that they need to:

- *Be open to criticism.*

- *Understand the trade offs they make – some negative comments are a part of doing business. Being perfect is too expensive.*

- *Be aware of blind spots — even if you are doing great, there may be some things that need improvement that are not "deal breakers" now, but make you vulnerable in the long run.*

- *An action plan starts with research, either by you or by a third party.*

- *Don't take action on any comment; take only measured reasonable action.*

- *Dealing with Hostile segment is especially important. The damage they can inflict is hard to predict.*

www.ingramcontent.com/pod-product-compliance
Lightning Source LLC
Chambersburg PA
CBHW031940190326
41519CB00007B/601